T0396257

pretty Little london

· EATS ·

pretty little london

· EATS ·

A GUIDE TO THE CITY'S BEST FOOD CULTURE

SARA SANTINI & ANDREA DI FILIPPO

FRANCES
LINCOLN

Contents

MORNING

BREAKFAST
10

BAKERIES
26

BRUNCH
38

AFTERNOON

LUNCH
58

STREET FOOD
86

PUBS
110

AFTERNOON TEA
128

EVENING

DRINKS
148

DINNER
176

INTRODUCTION

The foodie scene in London over the past ten years has gone from being good, to great, to *exceptional*. When we moved to London, back in 2014, never for one second did we we think that London could become a food destination, that people might visit it only for its incredible restaurants, fascinating food markets, sophisticated bars and vibrant pubs. But London does that, it surprises us all the time – and in many, myriad ways.

The celebration, in recent years, of London's immense cultural, ethnic and social diversity has been, we feel, as Italian observers living in England, a contributing factor to the vibrant explosion of the foodie scene. There are more than 140 different types of cuisine available in London alone, let alone other places around the nation – and that number is growing with more and more chefs bringing their regional dishes from their hometowns or homelands to the scene. Chefs are proudly bringing to the table flavours we've never tasted before, spices common to their cultures, but not necessarily widely known otherwise; they are celebrating their heritage and sharing secrets from across the world with us. It is possible to be transported to places far away just by smelling, seeing, tasting and trying these delicious morsels.

London's culinary diversity has shaped and brought business to neighbourhoods, with people visiting Brixton, for example, to try authentic Caribbean dishes, Brick Lane for the best curries in town and Clerkenwell for some of the best local Italian restaurants. With time, cultures and flavours have also started to blend, producing some fantastic fusion restaurants that celebrate different types of cuisine, rather than just one, and by doing so representing the diversity of its people.

Social media has also had a massive impact on the food scene, not just in London but around the world. Everyone takes pictures of their food. *Everyone*. Whether it's to boast about it on Instagram, to send to their family and friends or just to keep as a memory of that special something, we all love taking photos of our food. We just can't help ourselves. And we know that better than anyone. That's how we started, photographing places, people, food we'd experienced, and showing and sharing the places, restaurants and markets we loved on Instagram. That's where the *Pretty Little* series came from.

Social media is where people search for the best and coolest places to go. It has pushed chefs to get more creative with their dishes, especially presentation, in order to go viral on Instagram and TikTok, and all this without compromising on the quality of the food. It has incentivised restaurateurs to go big on the interiors, to create that picture-perfect spot that everyone will want to pose in front of. It has inspired people to travel the world and then return to their city, searching for that dish that can transport them back to the destination they've just visited. It has given people the opportunity to review restaurants and talk about them through their content without being a 'professional restaurant critic', something that would have been unthinkable even twenty years ago. Yes, social media has had a huge impact on London's food scene – and the global food scene, more generally.

Celebrity chefs have, of course, played a key role in encouraging people of all ages to aspire to become chefs, whether professional or decent homecooks, with supper clubs springing up in the remotest of places. And think of the global impact of TV shows like BBC's *MasterChef* franchise and *The Great British Bake Off*, showcasing how homecooks can become stars, many going on to open up their own restaurants and bakeries, or work in the best eateries in the world. Children once wanted to be astronauts and brain surgeons; today they want to become chefs. Netflix series, like *Chef's Table,* have inspired young chefs to pursue excellence, using local ingredients and travelling the world to discover new flavours. Everyone today wants to create something innovative in their kitchen. Everyone wants to use British ingredients to achieve greatness – from farm to table becoming ever more popular as the need to know what we're eating and its provenance increases in importance. And this has translated to international audiences, where restaurants and markets import UK ingredients sourced or grown here, such as award-winning cheeses, salmon, chocolate and alcohol in the form of whisky and UK-originated wines. So why not experience all that firsthand in the capital at some of the most interesting, historically important or architecturally beautiful food locations in the world?

In this book, we will guide you through the best way to make the most out of London's food scene, starting with breakfast, moving on to brunch, lunch and afternoon tea, and finishing off with drinks and dinner. Together, we will explore some of London's most influential culinary neighbourhoods and food markets.

We have tried to be as diverse in our book as the city, by including as many types of cuisine as possible and not limiting ourselves only to award-winning restaurants (there are many guides, the Michelin included, for that).

This is a personal selection, from two Italians who love London. We've included places that we think have a great vibe, great food, great staff, and so on – something that makes them stand out in a place full of fooderies. We have selected the very best locations – in our opinion – to make the most of every single moment of the day, whether it's hanging out at a Michelin-starred restaurant, a food truck in Camden Market, a neighbourhood pub in Notting Hill or a fancy bar in Mayfair.

With over 20,000 eateries in London today, it would have been impossible to try them all for this book, but hopefully we have given you an eclectic bucket list to follow and haven't left out too many of your favourites. If so, let us know. You know where we are.

But enough talking, let's eat!

MORNING

BREAKFAST

Duck & Waffle

24-HOUR BREAKFASTING WITH A VIEW

⊖ Liverpool Street

Fancy a breakfast with a view? Head up to the fortieth floor of the Salesforce tower in Liverpool Street and you'll find Duck & Waffle. With floor-to-ceiling windows and incredible panoramic views over the City, this is the best place in London for a sunrise breakfast.

If you are wondering where the name comes from, take a guess at what the ingredients of their signature dish are. The eponymous 'Duck & Waffle' is in fact a crispy leg confit with a big fried duck egg, sunny-side up, and mustard maple syrup, all on top of a big waffle. *Obviously.*

Vegetarians can enjoy a 'Wanne Be' Duck & Waffle made with a crispy hen of the woods mushroom tempura instead of the leg confit.

Among the many waffle options, we also recommend the sweet caramelised banana, made with 'housemade' hazelnut chocolate spread, vanilla ice cream and peanut crunch. What a dream.

Ducks and waffles apart, what makes this restaurant so unique is that it truly is open 24/7, something that's definitely not the norm in London! So, whether you're coming back from partying, you're in the mood for a midnight snack or you've simply decided to be brave and get up and watch the sunrise, this place is always open for you. And there's a branch in Edinburgh, too.

Eggslut

A KALEIDOSCOPE
OF GREAT EGGS

Various, see website

If you looove eggs, this is the place for you.

From its humble beginnings as a food truck, Eggslut has now grown to have numerous locations scattered around London, and globally. We think it's quite genius to have created a fast food that focuses uniquely on the humble egg. Quite frankly we are quite jealous we didn't think of it first.

Eggslut's shiny buns are perfect for a breakfast on the go – just make sure you bring loads of tissues with you, as this can be a messy affair. Favourite dishes include the Fairfax, with scrambled eggs, caramelised onions, sriracha mayo and cheese, and the Portobello Truffle. The wait can be long but watching the chefs at work, scrambling away in the huge pots and pans is a fun distraction and, once you get your hands on those warm buns, you'll even forget you had to queue.

The Breakfast Club

A 'CAF' CRAZY FOR PANCAKES

⊖ Various, see website

These cute little cafs – 'cafs', as the owners are keen to stress, not cafés or cafés – are dotted all over the city and, with their distinguished egg yolk yellow façades, they truly brighten up any London neighbourhood. It doesn't matter which one you go to, whether the Islington branch, London Bridge or the Soho ones (just to name a few), you'll be greeted by the same friendly service and feel-good comfort food.

Founded by two best friends from Yorkshire, these 'cafs' are now beloved London institutions, managing to put an end to any 'where should we go for breakfast?' discussion, the irritating ones we all have at some point. With an expansive choice of food – from the Full Monty and Greasy Spoon English to various Benedicts and ubiquitous smashed avocado – and the option to swap any meat items with delicious vegan alternatives – The Breakfast Club makes everybody happy.

This is also the place to go if you are crazy for pancakes. Order the Pancakes, Cream & Berries stack, if you have a sweet tooth. Or the savoury All American, which comes with the most delicious crispy homestyle potatoes. And don't forget a side of French toast fingers made to dip perfectly in to maple syrup, made to share.

. . . Or not to share. We'll leave that up to you!

Fischer's

A VIENNESE-STYLE GRAND CAFÉ IN MARYLEBONE

⊖ Baker Street

Fischer's is a much-loved neighbourhood restaurant located in gorgeous Marylebone. Inspired by those European grand cafés, the menu proudly highlights classic Viennese dishes, such as insanely big schnitzels, decadent sachertorte with apricot jam, kaiserschmarrns (literally 'imperial mess', a fluffy, shredded pancake) and Käsekrainer (a lightly smoked Brühwurst, filled with pieces of cheese).

For breakfast, along with classics staples, such as yogurt with Birchmüsli (so simple yet so good) or eggs Benedict, you can find Austrian specialities, with the likes of sweet potato röstis and gröstls, with paprika fried potatoes and fried eggs making an appearance. Or why not try a smoked salmon and cream cheese pretzel, a Fischer's favourite? Simply delicious!

Don't forget to add an item of Viennoiserie, and if you want to kick-start your morning with a bit sugar you can pick a warm apple strudel or a Black Forest gâteau from the Konditorei section of the tea menu, to go with your Fischer's hot chocolate, of course.

On a sunny day, try to snag a table outside. There are only two, so this could be quite the challenge and yet it's so worth trying! Trust us – this is a heavenly slice of Vienna in a lovely part of central London.

+ INSIDER TIP
〰〰〰〰〰

Add the pink grapefruit to your order – for health reasons, or maybe just because it has the prettiest presentation, peeled to perfection and served in gorgeous silverware over ice.

Katsute 100

JAPANESE PATISSERIE AND MATCHA HEAVEN

⊖ Angel

Bored of eggs and pancakes for breakfast? We feel you. Sometimes you just want something delicate and to sip on a hot tea while working on your laptop or just to have a moment of calm, watching people pass by. Katsute 100 Islington is just the place to do so.

Nestled in pretty Camden Passage, this traditional Japanese tearoom serves Matcha and many ceremonial teas the right way, using artisan and specialist suppliers to provide an interesting array. Antique wooden Japanese furniture, vintage artwork and decorative saké bottles make the inside space harmonious, while the charming back garden provides a true escape from the ouside world. It's not by chance that the word katsute means nostalgia, a true 'once upon a time' feel.

We love coming up here in the morning to work away undisturbed or to sit outside enjoying some delightful homemade traditional Japanese cakes. The Matcha crêpe cake and the strawberry shortcake are some of the most chosen, but they also experiment with European flavours that are quite popular in Japan. And visit during sakura (cherry blossom) season in late March/early April, you'll be pleased to find special Matcha flavours and themed-pink delicacies.

M
O
R
N
I
N
G

Regency Café

A TRUE BRITISH EXPERIENCE FROM THE PAST

⊖ Pimlico

The Regency Café first opened its doors in 1946 in the eponymous London street in Pimlico. This greasy spoon serves fry-ups and proper builder's tea for what seems twentieth-century prices, a rarity in such an inflating economy!

The interiors are designed in an Art Deco style with original white tiles, and its chequered little curtains make it for an irresistible photo opportunity. No wonder it was been used as a backdrop in fashion shoots, TV programmes and movies, including *Layer Cake* and *Pride*. In reality, this humble, no-frills British café is fashionable without trying. When dining here there is only one thing you should order and that's the Full English Breakfast. Coming with thick, white buttered bread or toast, why not also throw in delicious hash browns or chips? Go on, you know you want to!

The service is fast, the queues long. Be prepared to be yelled at if you break the number one rule of claiming a table before placing your order at the counter.

Is it worth it? Absolutely.

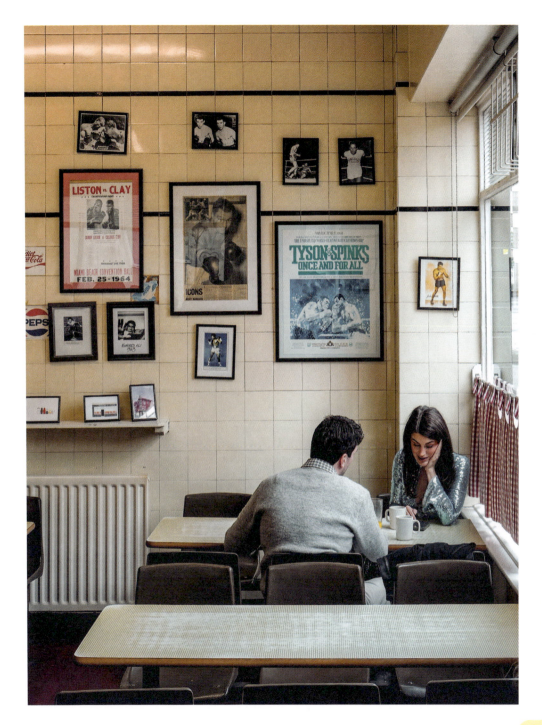

Pavilion Café
Victoria Park

SRI LANKAN FARE ON AN
EAST LONDON WATERFRONT

⊖ Bethnal Green/Mile End

If you are looking for your next breakfast spot for a sunny weekend, then look no further. This incarnation of the Pavilion Café (there are several) is set in lovely Victoria Park, overlooking the lake, and it makes for the perfect start of day before a wander around the glories of east London.

This bustling bakery serves not only freshly baked pastries but also delicious Sri Lankan-inspired breakfast goodies, a menu born of former social worker–owner Rob Green's love of the country from his time spent volunteering at an orphanage there. You will always find house chai brewing behind the till – Rob had a successful tea stall in Borough and Broadway markets – and hearty bowls of Sri Lankan dhal and sambol at lunchtime, ready to be devoured by hungry locals and visitors alike. The tasty Swedish-style buns are made with spices like cardamom, cinnamon and turmeric.

Dog- and kid-friendly, everyone is welcome in this east London institution.

+ INSIDER TIP
〰〰〰〰

Grab a warm loaf of its renowned sourdough bread or homemade granola while you're there.

The River Restaurant
by Gordon Ramsay

A WATERSIDE BREAKFAST
AT THE SAVOY

⊖ Charing Cross/Embankment

The River Restaurant is set in the iconic Savoy hotel, a venue that really needs no introduction! Open to everybody, not only hotel guests, this is a stylish yet relaxed, beautiful restaurant which gives you access to luxury life without having to stay overnight. Unless you want to.

We tried the Quintessentially English Breakfast, which comes at a pricey £24, at time of writing. Of course it has all the trimmings – streaky bacon, sausages, black pudding, tomato, mushrooms, baked beans and eggs, cooked just how you like them. Some people say, however, that when having breakfast at The Savoy there is only one thing to order: the Omelette Arnold Bennett. Made with Comté cheese, Parmesan and smoked haddock, this particular egg dish was invented in honour of the author who was a guest of the hotel in 1929. And we will be the first ones to throw a tantrum if it's ever taken off the menu.

+ INSIDER TIP
〰〰〰〰〰

Whatever you order, make sure to ask for a table by the window – breakfast with a side of River Thames views. What's more London?

45 Jermyn St.

BREAKFAST IN TRUE STYLE

⬛ Green Park/Piccadilly Circus

Nothing says elegance quite like Jermyn Street. Home to London's finest menswear fashion brands, this is where old-school shirtmakers and tailors mingle with luxury designers and independent boutiques.

Jermyn Street really is a paradise to all dandies and fashionistas who enjoy a bit of shopping, for British heritage brands especially. In this charming location, nestled in a corner spot between Jermyn Street and Fortnum & Mason, you will find 45 Jermyn St., standing proud with its bright orange shades and light green façade. Even though the interior plush terracotta booths might look tempting, we recommend taking a seat outside.

The area is truly a prime people-watching spot – we are in Jermyn Street after all. There is something quite romantic about spying well-dressed passers-by and loyal clients starting their day here, magazine in one hand, coffee of choice in the other. Foodwise, you can expect to find classic breakfast staples, including freshly squeezed juices, yummy granola and pastries. Scrambled eggs are pimped up with caviar at 45 Jermyn St. – quite frankly we expected nothing less.

Breakfast is available from 7:30 a.m. on weekdays, and from 8 a.m. at the weekend, until 11 a.m. each day.

E Pellicci is really a place like no other. Located in Bethnal Green and still owned by the same family, this little café has been making breakfast for Londoners since 1900. Thanks to its charm and authenticity, this remains one of the most extraordinary places, in our opinion, in the city. Loved by locals and tourists alike, who travel to eat here, it was once a favoured spot of London gangsters, the Kray twins, who reportedly came here every morning growing up and as adults, as it was close to their home in Vallance Road. The atmosphere is loud, fun and vibrant, making you feel right at home.

Originally from Italy, Elide – who put the E in Pellicci – and her husband set up shop here, buying it from the original owner and living above the premises. Elide brought up their seven children single-handed after her husband's death, while running the café, until her son took control of the shop. Today Maria Nevio, Elide's daughter-in-law, is the head of the family business and together with son Nevio, Jr, daughter Anna and their cousin/ nephew Tony, they keep the tradition alive. Although not breakfast, make sure to try Maria's incredible homemade bread pudding, Nutella roly-poly and the other delicacies which she has made by hand, since the mid-1960s.

Even though the family originates from Italy and there are classic dishes on the menu, E Pellicci is really a place to go for a Full English Breakfast! With eggs, sausages, bacon, mushrooms, black pudding, beans, tomatoes and fried bread on offer (there is a vegetarian option), their portions are so generous you certainly won't leave hungry.

Today, along with locals, many celebrities pop in for breakfast to pay a visit to this iconic spot, which has also been awarded Grade-II listed status thanks to its history. Chances are there will be a queue, especially at weekends, but it's really worth it!

E Pellicci

BREAKFAST WHERE
THE KRAYS ONCE ATE

⊖ Bethnal Green

+ INSIDER TIP

Ask Anna to bring out a jar of her homemade pesto to dip your chips in. Just trust us on this!

The Wolseley

LONDON'S FIRST GRAND CAFÉ

⊖ Green Park/Piccadilly Circus

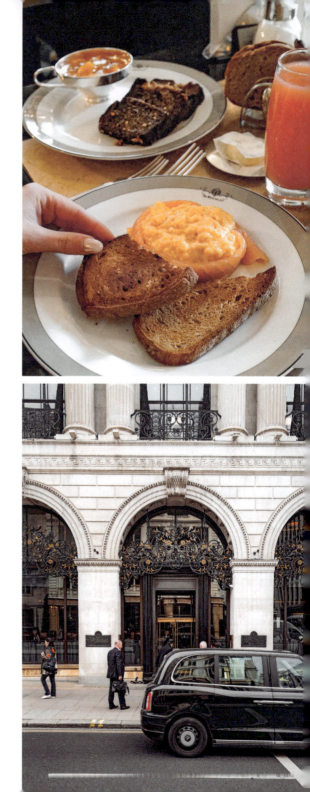

The Wolseley is really what comes to our mind when we think of a great historic venue in which to enjoy breakfast in the capital, with a great location and European-inspired menu. Set just a stone's throw from Green Park, between the Ritz and Fortnum's, this magnificent building was once the showroom of British car brand Wolseley Motors. Full of distinguished people enjoying breakfast before work on weekdays, and with cheerful tourists and locals at the weekend, this grand café is worth experiencing.

While the impressive green marble pillars and Florentine-inspired archways weren't enough to sell cars and the company fell quickly into bankruptcy, only for Barclays Bank to take it, The Wolseley now combines the best of British with European flair, a fact also seen on its menu.

Our usual is pink grapefruit juice, scrambled eggs or an omelette cooked to perfection and an unmissable item of Viennoiserie (the pain aux raisins and banana bread with jam are superb). As expected, the Wolseley also has a fine selection of British classics, from boiled eggs with soldiers, to grilled kippers, fried haggis with duck eggs and, of course, devilled kidneys, the kind of fare you might expect when weekending at a friend's stately home. And all this in the centre of bustling Piccadilly!

+ INSIDER TIP
〰〰〰〰

Breakfast starts at 7 a.m. on weekdays and
8 a.m. at the weekend, and is served until 11:30 a.m.

Camden Market

Camden Market is an exciting destination that anybody visiting London has to see at least once. Opened in 1974, with just sixteen stalls, it was originally a temporary market, only open one day a week. Its popularity grew fast. Now the largest market in London, there are over one thousand stalls, varying from fashion, vintage, homeware and, of course, loads of foodie options, celebrating the old and the new.

In the nineteenth century, the whole industrial Camden Lock served as a distillery for a world-renowned gin and some of the historic buildings can still be seen today around the market. In 2014, Half Hitch Gin brought back to life the distilling tradition of Camden Market, installing a micro-distillery in Camden Lock's West Yard, right next to the former gin warehouse. It is open to visitors, so if you are interested in the process of distilling and the history of gin, this is a good place to start your visit.

Looking for something to eat can be quite overwhelming, with so many great options available. What you need to know to get about is that the market is essentially divided into three areas: the Stables, Camden Lock and the newest, Hawley Wharf.

The Stables is the most historic area of the market. This labyrinth of alleys and arches once was the home of horse stables, saddlers and even a horse hospital. It now features an Insta-worthy alley of independent stores set under a roof of colourful umbrellas and cobbled yards, with the majority of experiences dine-in restaurants and takeaway stalls. Here, you can find absolutely everything that tickles your fancy – from incredible vegan burger at V Burger to the fun Funky Chips. Head to Farrier for rustic modern dining, and Italian craft beers

at Baladin Camden if you are looking for indoor seating. For sweets, queue at the popular 7 Heaven for chocolate-y Dutch poffertjes, head to Chin Chin labs to try their signature hot chocolate with torched gooey marshmallows or enter the magical world of Hans & Gretel for an OTT experience.

The Camden Lock area, the original location of the market, is where you'll find the most viral and experimental street foods stalls. Located right by Regent's Canal, there aren't many seats available here but you can join everybody else and sit wherever you find a suitable spot, which may be right on the ground. From the groundbreaking 3D-printed vegan steaks from Steakhaus (a must try) to a whole British roast in a burrito by Yorkshire Burritos and Venezuelan wraps by the Arepazo Bros, it's impossible only to pick one. But do you need to?

Hawley Wharf, set in the railway arches on the other side of the road, is the more modern area of the market. It features a Curzon cinema, independent retailers and a covered food court. It's right here that you'll see A'do'RE fritto, where you can grab famous Italian streetfood specialities such as Montanarina fritta (fried pizza dough topped with tomato sauce and cheese) or folded fried pizza with provola. To cleanse the palate, head to Japanese Tsujiri, the destination for Kyoto-inspired desserts and soft serve Matcha ice creams.

All of these foodie options should keep you occupied for a day – or week even – so make sure you reserve plenty of time and an empty stomach for your visit to Camden Market. And if in doubt, try one of the Secret Food Tours – an easy introduction to some of the market's hidden gems.

MORNING

BAKERIES

Arôme Bakery

A FRENCH PATISSERIE WITH A JAPANESE TWIST

Covent Garden/Leicester Square

+ INSIDER TIP

Hang around for long enough, in front of the outside window, and you'll spy the pastry chefs doing their dance, cutting up the chunky Shokupan into perfectly symmetrical squares, all ready to be prettied up for you to enjoy.

This cute independent bakery in Seven Dials, Covent Garden, has won everybody over in the last couple of years. While it offers traditional patisserie, such as flaky tartes fine aux pommes and buttery croissants made using age-old French techniques, Arôme's unique selling point is its Asian-inspired pastries. Creations like the Miso Bacon Escargot (the shape of it, not snails!) or the pistachio chocolate equivalent, and Gula Melaka Coconut Twist are popular countertop sellers, along with Arôme's special seasonally flavoured goodies.

The star of the show is, without any doubt, the signature Arôme Honey Butter Toast, made from a thick slice of Japanese traditional Shokupan (Japanese milk bread), enveloped in a caramelised honey crust. The result is a crispy on the surface, but soft and fluffy on the inside, little square of joy. What more do you want?

MORNING

Chestnut Bakery

EAST MEETS WEST

⊖ Covent Garden/Victoria

With locations, as we type, in Belgravia and Covent Garden, Kuwait-originated Chestnut Bakery came alive when co-founder Ahmad started supplying a number of restaurants with delicious pastries and breads from his ghost kitchen. His very first branch opened in Elizabeth Street, Belgravia and shortly after he set up shop in gorgeous Floral Street, Covent Garden. Keeping the Middle Eastern influence and flavours, the Chestnut Bakery has created an array of tasty and fragrant pastries and breads, made by its skilful bakers, to mass appeal.

Choosing what to order between all the picture-perfect pastries can be a daunting task, so good luck trying to pick only one! The plain croissant – elected Best Croissant in the UK in 2023 – has been adapted to numerous variations, including the crowd-pleaser plant-based pistachio and raspberry. If you prefer more savoury options, ingredients include kimchi, labneh, za'atar and truffle. Yummy!

There is also always a fun monthly seasonal special. Our personal favourite is the Honey Toast – which remains a constant on the menu – and is made with toasted croissant topped with geymar (a delicious Iraqi clotted cream), honeycomb and a drizzle of honey.

+ INSIDER TIP
〰〰〰〰

The outside sitting areas are just lovely in both locations, but if the weather is not so nice, head inside to the second floor for a stunning view over Floral Street in the Covent Garden branch.

Chai Guys Bakehouse

INDIAN FUSION PASTRIES

⊖ Notting Hill Gate/Westbourne Grove

With chai stalls in Old Spitalfields Market and Seven Dials, popular Chai Guys Bakehouse has set up store in fashionable Notting Hill's Portobello and it's the perfect location to do so. Using the best of ingredients, it's upgraded what we think of Indian 'chai' and serves three types of high-quality 50/50 spice-to-tea ratio blends. Customers have a choice of: Masala or Kadak, both with CTC black tea at their base, and Kashmiri tea, which uses green tea instead of black, although it's strikingly and naturally pink in colour!

Chai Guys Bakehouse's pastries are inspired by Japanese baking techniques, made with Indian spices and seasonal British ingredients. Sounds like a bit of a mouthful but it works so well. Think cardamom-infused chai spice milk bread accompanied with a touch of salted butter, miso mushroom rolls and Gujarati dhoklas – savoury sponge cakes, served with green chilli coriander chutney. Just delightful. These spiced baked goods are switched around quite quickly so that people always have something interesting to discover.

Wash it all down with your iconic spiced chai blend of choice. You know, typical Chai Guys stuff.

+ INSIDER TIP
〜〜〜〜〜

Pick up some handblended chai and make your own at home. It won't be the same but it'll be a reminder of how great Chai Guys is!

Layla Bakery

A NEIGHBOURHOOD ARTISAN BAKERY WITH A TWIST

Ladbroke Grove

Enter Layla, the Ladbroke Grove artisan bakery which commands down-the-street lines every single morning. Everything is freshly baked here, made right in front of you, using only seasonal ingredients, wild grains and ancient traditions.

We were lucky enough to visit Layla before trading hours to get a sneak peek at its operation and we thought it was going to be the calm before the storm, but, oh boy, we were wrong! The pastry preparation was in full swing and the chefs were moving together in sync like an orchestra. Some were rolling dough behind the counter, some were dusting and knotting and some were putting together the very last details, all the while talking to each other in what seemed like a secret language. Not a finished pastry in sight and we were five minutes away from opening, yet all was calm. Filling the counter before the customers arrived looked like an impossible task, yet within minutes everything came together like magic.

As for what's on show, expect a rotation of seasonal pastries and beloved classics. We sat on the shared benches outside, watching Ladbroke Grove's bustle, and tried the gianduja bow tie croissants, an iconic piece really, the pistachio pain Suisse and the seasonal rhubarb crème fraîche. What a dream! And if you're in the mood for something savoury, there's a lot to choose from – garlic croissants, wonderful sandwiches and sourdough among them.

Greedy Cow Bakes

THE FLUFFIEST KOREAN MILK DOUGHNUTS IN LONDON

⊖ Cambridge Heath

Meet the east London bakery that is making locals, or the whole of London to be fair, stand in line for hours, rain or shine. This Hackney Road wonder was one of those successful lockdown projects which turned into a thriving business. Founder Nazia Jasmin quickly had to turn from baking in her home kitchen to finding business premises, so popular were her delicious wares.

Now, the demand is so high that even though the number of doughnuts they bake increases constantly, they sell through – and quickly – every single day. In terms of flavours, you can find crème brûlée, Victoria sponge or Ferrero Rocher amongst others, but the real MVP are those fluffy Korean milk doughnuts they've become famous for, filled with whipped cream and light as air! Seriously, out of this world.

Situated close to the Columbia Road Flower Market, once you have tasted a Greedy Cow Bakes good, you won't be able to walk past the shop without stopping for a little sweet treat. No matter how much those flowers are calling.

+ INSIDER TIP
〰〰〰〰〰

Come super early, and be prepared to queue.

Fortitude Bakehouse

VIRAL BEIGNETS WORTH QUEUING FOR

Russell Square

Meet Fortitude Bakehouse. A tiny bakery hidden away in a cobbled mews in Bloomsbury's Russell Square. It's taken London by social media storm with its fragrant Middle Eastern flavours and light-as-air *beignets* (deep-fried, fluffy doughnut-like pastries).

Be ready to queue, but the line is worth it! Behind the charming blue façade you'll discover all kinds of baked goods, including savoury buns, delectable scones and the popular almond and orange blossom water bearclaws, as well as the much-lauded star of the show, beignets. One of the first bakeries to make them in London, it has now evolved from the classic cream kind and have moved on to more interesting flavours, such as blueberry, maple and cardamom, Black Forest and coffee.

There are no seats inside and only a couple of benches out so, since you'll probably get your lovely food to take away, remember to squeeze in the back and grab a few (or a lot) of napkins. Eating can be a bit of a messy job.

+ INSIDER TIP

The beignets only come out at 11 a.m. daily and are available until they sell out. Once there are gone . . . they are gone!

Pophams

NEIGHBOURHOOD FAVOURITE

🚇 Angel

Considered one of the best bakeries in town, this artisanal store prides itself on using traditional techniques and the absolute best seasonal ingredients.

Pophams has now branched out into London Fields and Victoria Park, as we write, but the original Islington flagship remains an iconic north London institution, adored by locals and visitors alike. Its handcrafted Viennoiserie pastries are seriously to die for, and here we probably tasted the best pain au chocolate of our lives. Apart from the classics, Pophams offers pastries with an innovative spin, imagined by creator Ollie Gold and his knowledge of all things baked goods, learnt through his travels.

So, want to keep things interesting? Try the honey and smoked salt bun, bacon and maple swirl or seasonal specials such as rhubarb and cardamom custard, all fresh out of the oven. And if you're in love with the pretty ceramic plates and coffee mugs you've just dined off, good news, they're for sale. Made by local artisans, we love them so much, we have to leave with a cup or two every time we visit! A little slice of Pophams in our home.

MORNING

Yeast Bakery

CROISSANT SWIRLS AND
BRIOCHE FEUILLETÉES

🚇 Bethnal Green

In east London, just steps away from Broadway Market and close to leafy London Fields, is a real gem of the London bakery scene. It's here, right by the Regent's Canal, that sweet-toothed Londoners will find the blush pink-coloured Yeast Bakery, a place that started in 2011 with the aim of making the perfect croissant.

Now its popularity is arguably down to its brioche feuilletées and circle swirls, a familiar sight to viral audiences. The former is a tall, layered brioche filled with the likes of cinnamon and salted caramel or raspberry and cream, and is a twist on a classic; seriously too good to be true. The latter resembles a croissant wheel and is made with interesting toppings and inventive combinations such as Matcha and white chocolate, tiramisu or Biscoff and vanilla mascarpone. Both pastries are generously filled with smooth cream and are crunchy on the bite and light and airy on the inside; just how we like them.

Other decadent in-house creations include the Croaf▉ – a croissant loaf essentially – and kouign-amann, a small, round caramelised sweet-buttery treat which it makes perfectly. Co-founders Angela and Ben have succeeded in creating the perfect little family-owned bakery, both inviting and beautifully designed. And if that's not enough, you can dine here on freshly made sourdough toasties, various egg dishes and sandwiches, among other things. The perfect place to brunch. And then shop.

Jolene

HERITAGE GRAINS
AND HOMEMADE
PASTRIES ON
THE GO

Angel

This charming Angel bakery, little sister of the original branch in Newington Green, is the perfect place to grab a coffee on the go and a delicious pastry or two. The cute branded yellow cups and rusty orange façade make it irresistible not to go in. Jolene's carby goodies are seriously top-notch, with the emphasis on sustainability and provenance: more than fifty grains going into the flour it uses, most grown by Groove Armada's Andy Cato. No wonder this bakery is so highly regarded!

Freshly baked every day, with a changing blackboard menu, the croissants, pain au chocolate and cakes are proudly lined up on the counter, ready to lure you. Seasonality is a big thing at Jolene, so do expect pumpkin-infused delicacies in autumn and rhubarb-flavoured bakes in spring. Quality and taste are important to Jolene.

M
O
R
N
I
N
G

Chinatown

Pretty much every country has a Chinatown in its major cities and London's is among the best known. Situated in central London in Gerrard Street and its immediate environs between Soho and theatreland, it's a thriving hub full of restaurants, bakeries, supermarkets, shops, bars and much more.

The site of Chinese New Year and other celebrations, tourists flock to the area to enjoy its food. But what if we told you that Chinatown was once elsewhere in London?

From the late eighteenth century onwards, Chinese sailors arrived at Limehouse in east London, courtesy of the East India Company, which imported tea, silks and spices. Migration increased in the nineteenth century, although the population remained in the hundreds, with some Chinese deciding to settle in the docklands. This area became the site of the first Chinatown as people opened businesses, usually restaurants, shops and laundries to supplement their income. Limehouse retained its status until the Second World War, when east London was heavily bombed during the Blitz and Chinatown was all but destroyed.

During the 1950s, the Chinese community found another 'town' in Soho, which had a reputation of having low rent (unimaginable today!). It gained a reputation, thanks to the British soldiers who had fallen in love with local food during their campaigns in China and Japan. As success attracts success, many more Chinese entrepreneurs started to open businesses on Gerrard Street, and by the late 1960s the Chinatown that we know and love today was born.

By the 1980s red lanterns and Chinese gates started to adorn the streets, and Gerrard Street, parts of Newport Place and Macclesfield Street were pedestrianised, becoming a home away from home for people from the Chinese community and those enjoying the culture and food.

Today, Chinatown has become a full-on foodie destination. Until the early 2000s, most of the food offered in this area was Chinese. But things have changed. Now you will find Malaysian, Korean, Singaporean and Thai food, in addition to regional Sichuan, Cantonese and Gansu dishes. Desserts have also been booming in the past few years, with new trends from Asia finding their way to London's streets, to the extent that Chinatown has its very own 'dessert alley' in Newport Court, where you can find anything from fish-shaped waffles, Matcha soft serve, Hong Kong-style egg waffles to Filipino ice cream stuffed into buns and bubble tea Basque cheesecake.

One of our favourite restaurants here is Orient, owned by one of the oldest families in Chinatown. It serves authentic, freshly cooked food, with dim sum, noodles, steamed lava buns, fried rice and more. Other favourites are Plum Valley and Jinli, and for bao buns definitely head to Bun House, which serves both savoury and sweet steamed buns – the egg custard is to die for!

For those of you with a sweet tooth, a must-stop is the iconic Chinatown Bakery to pick up one of their famous fish-shaped waffles, filled with gooey custard paste, made at the window with their Taiyaki machine. We also really love Héfaure for their Japanese soufflé pancakes and the Japanese cake boutique Sakurado, just next door.

SAKURADO **①**

HÉFAURE **③**

CHINATOWN BAKERY **④**

PLUM VALLEY **②**

⑤ BUN HOUSE

⑥ JINLI

⑦ ORIENT

Leicester Square

Piccadilly Circus

+ INSIDER TIP
〰〰〰〰

The event that most people look forward to in Chinatown is definitely Chinese New Year. The date changes every year, depending on the lunar cycle, and the festival lasts around two weeks, so you will need to check beforehand when the festivities commence. Be sure to drop by, as you will find colourful parades, spectacular stage performances, dragon dances and much more.

M O R N I N G

MORNING

BRUNCH

26 Grains

A COSY SCANDI EXPERIENCE FOR PORRIDGE LOVERS

Covent Garden

Hidden in colourful Neal's Yard – right by Covent Garden's Seven Dials – is 26 Grains, a cute little café with an irresistible pastel blue façade. Inspired by founder's Alex's regular travels to Copenhagen, it is based around seasonality, which is at the centre of the Danish way of living and eating. A feeling of cosiness pervades Scandinavian culture and what better than having a warm bowl of porridge in the colder months to say exactly that?

As you might expect from the name, the majority of things on the menu are based around grains, so think an array of sweets and savoury porridges, rye sandwiches and breads. We love the five-grain porridge with banana, tahini, honey, cinnamon and cacao nibs and the pear and tumeric, but we are on a mission to try all of their flavours. It might take a while, but we are certainly up for the challenge!

Christopher's

THE BEST FRENCH TOAST IN TOWN, WE PROMISE!

⊖ Charing Cross/Covent Garden

Regarded as one of London's best modern American restaurants, Christopher's can be found standing proud in bustling Covent Garden. Founded in 1991, this restaurant is set in a magnificent Grade II-listed building, once home to a papier-mâché factory and then to London's first licensed casino.

Striving to maintain this allure of old-school glamour, Christopher's compromises three spaces – a Martini Bar on the ground floor, a dining room on the first floor and, in true American style, a speakeasy Club Room for private events only on the lower ground floor. The weekend brunch offering, from 11 a.m. until 3 p.m., showcases an array of American flavours and classic dishes, such as pecan pie with salted caramel ice cream, honeycomb New York cheesecake and lobster mac'n'cheese.

The Stateside-style menu also offers plenty of creative mains, such as the egg Maryland – a crab cake twist on the eggs Benedict – the huevos California, with tortilla, chilli salsa and Monterey Jack cheese, and C's pink sauce rigatoni. Now, what you absolutely should not miss is the chocolate brioche French toast. Coming with milk or dark warm chocolate sauce to drizzle over the slices and vanilla ice cream, this is no doubt one of the best French toasts in town. If not the best. There, we said it!

Tab x Tab

AN INSTA-WORTHY BRUNCH

Notting Hill Gate

Tab x Tab is a small independent brunch spot, just off Notting Hill, which has received quite the attention for its picture-perfect brunch dishes. Your classic avo on toast here comes with faultless swirls of coriander, cashew and avocado paste, with the possibility of adding a spicy szechuan oil, which not only looks adorable, but more importantly tastes delicious too. The indulgent French toast is served with pistachio namelaka – a smooth Japanese style of ganache – fresh strawberries and a generous sprinkle of almond crumble.

If you fancy some eggs, the sourdough with scrambled eggs and creamy mushrooms is always a hit and it comes in a very generous portion. A vegan option ia banana pancakes with a cloud of blueberry lime compote and maple pecan butter. Dangerously addictive!

If that's not enough sweetness for you, on the way out be sure to pick up one of their freshly baked cakes and biscuits from the counter. Great to enjoy later! On a beautiful sunny day, take a seat at the outdoor benches and, if the weather is not so nice, cosy up on one of the window stools, with a flat white, or two, and watch the world go by.

MORNING

Lantana

AUSSIE BRUNCH PIONEERS

🚇 Goodge Street/London Bridge/Old Street

This is the place to go for the original Aussie brunch. Lantana was one of the first places to bring a taste of the country to London. On the menu you can expect healthy goodness and fresh dishes in line with the 'Down Under' lifestyle and culture.

The decadent mushroom Benedict and corn fritters with halloumi and poached eggs are brunch staples at Lantana, and they come much recommended by the team. They also have both savoury and sweet French toasts on the menu – such as a chicken Karaage (Japanese fried chicken) with chilli and maple syrup and a French toast topped with elderflower-poached peaches, berries, lemon cream and a nutty crumble.

At the weekend, you can enjoy a Hold the Booze bottomless brunch for £39, with unlimited coffee and juices, or a less abstemious Lantana Blowout, complete with endless Mimosas or prosecco for £49. There are currently branches in Shoreditch, London Bridge and Fizrovia, the original Lantana, where it all began.

Capilungo

This Italian café in Covent Garden transports you to the beautiful streets of Lecce in Puglia. Run by brother and sister team Asia and Gianluca Capilungo, with the help of their savvy uncle, Luca who has been running his bakery in the Italian town since 1991, we guess you could call it a family affair.

The décor of the café is pastel peach and green, to match the colours of this beautiful city, often called 'The Florence of the South'. The main feature on the menu is the 'pasticciotto Leccese', which ticks all the boxes for what we feel a perfect pastry should look like: it's creamy with a bit of crispiness from the pastry – and, of course, it's deliciously sweet. The Caffe Leccese is also a must try, made out of homemade almond syrup, coffee and ice. It's almost a ritual for locals in Puglia, something to enjoy on those very hot summer days.

Capilungo also serves a delicious puff pastry named *rustico* and other artisan, freshly baked goodies, with many of these ingredients sourced directly from Luca's suppliers in Lecce. Noteworthy is also the pistachio hot chocolate, made with white chocolate and topped with cream and crushed pistachios. Grab the best seat in the house – by the window – and people-watch with a warm *pasticciotto* in your hands.

If all this isn't enough to convince you to visit this café, stay on or visit at night to experience a completely different ambience – it turns into a wine bar, where you can catch up with friends over a glass of Primitivo. Or two.

Caravan

A WELL-TRAVELLED MENU AND PROPER, GOOD COFFEE

⊖ Farringdon

These trusty restaurants, scattered around central London, are always great when it comes to brunch and are definitely a hit among London visitors. Started by three Kiwi friends who were missing the relaxed coffee house culture of New Zealand, Caravan counts, as we type, eight branches in the city. Not bad for some friends that were just missing a good old cup of coffee! The original location was founded, in 2010, in Exmouth Market, with the idea that people could come in the morning and hang around as long as they wanted until it was time to swap the coffee for a cocktail or two.

The relaxed atmosphere makes it the perfect place for brunch with friends, a work meeting or drinks after work. The all-day menu is, as they say, 'well-travelled' and includes international flavours and dishes, such as the garam masala spiced French toast, jalapeño cornbread with fried eggs, mojo verde and chilli butter and poached eggs with whipped yoghurt, fenugreek chilli butter, gunpowder and flatbread.

Have we made you hungry yet?

+ INSIDER TIP
〜〜〜〜〜〜〜

We like the original branch on Exmouth Market, as there are independent shops to visit afterwards.

The Buttery

RUSTIC-CHIC
BRUNCH

Victoria

The Buttery, set inside the pretty Lime Tree Hotel in Belgravia, has quickly become one of our favourite sports for brunch in London. Its eggs are truly divine, and the charming rustic-chic interiors and walled garden have you covered, whatever the weather.

Between the country garden, egg yolks as red as they can possibly be and paintings with horses and dogs, this cosy restaurant is a taste of the Cotswolds, but in central London. Nods to the countryside are all over the menu too, with dishes such as the Allotment Breakfast, a veggie breakfast made with grilled halloumi, spiced smashed avocado, all the trimmings of an English Breakfast and Cacklebean eggs cooked as you like them.

When brunching at the Buttery there is one thing you really shouldn't miss and that's its Nutella French toast. Leave some space for this indulgent delicacy made with mascarpone and cherry compote crème, maple syrup and a sprinkle of toasted hazelnuts. You'll thank us later.

MORNING

Madera

MEXICAN BRUNCH FIESTA

⊖ Oxford Circus/Piccadilly Circus

Are tacos and huevos rancheros your dream brunch? Do you go crazy for Bloody Marys and spicy margaritas? Well, if you haven't made your way up to Madera on Regent Street, you are definitely missing out!

Located on the fifteenth floor of the Treehouse London hotel, this elevated Mexican restaurant offers a different take on brunch. Along with sweeping views across the city, you can expect huge taco and quesadilla boards, designed to share and be filled up with your choices of meats, vegan chicken and vegetables. Along with a full vegan menu, you can also find flavoursome Mexican–Californian classics such as huevos rancheros and enfrijoladas, a thee-corn tortilla dish filled with eggs made the Mexican way, cheese and refried beans. For dessert, the Madera churros with warm chocolate sauce are seriously to die for. Don't forget about drinks though, here at Madera there is a whole dedicated Bloody Mary station where you can pimp up your drinks with an array of spices, garnishes and sauces. It's such fun and we loved feeling like a bartender for the day!

Apple Butter Café

EAT BRUNCH
AROUND AN
APPLE TREE

Covent Garden

Apple Butter Café in Monmouth Street, Seven Dials, is very welcoming, decorated with an archway of flowers on the storefront and cosy red bricks and a wooden floor on the inside.

A spectacular apple tree takes centre stage in the dining room, for all to admire, creating an oasis of calm from busy London. If it's a sunny day, you can sit outside at one of the marble-topped tables, which is exactly what we did. The food is bright, fun and picture-perfect, as well as being so incredibly good. The stack of incredible signature pancakes change flavour daily, so it's always fun to come back and see what's in store. We got Black Forest, made with a rich chocolate sauce and cherry compote. So indulgent! The croissant butter pudding is also unmissable, made with a warm drizzle of custard, torn pieces of baked croissant and pecan nuts.

And that's not all – the all-day menu also includes the likes of truffle scrambled eggs on brioche, eggs Florentine with pink beetroot hollandaise and avo halloumi toast. All great brunch dishes. There is also an array of warming signature drinks, such as Biscoff and crème brûlée lattes. You might need a full day to burn all that off, but it's well worth the calories!

MORNING

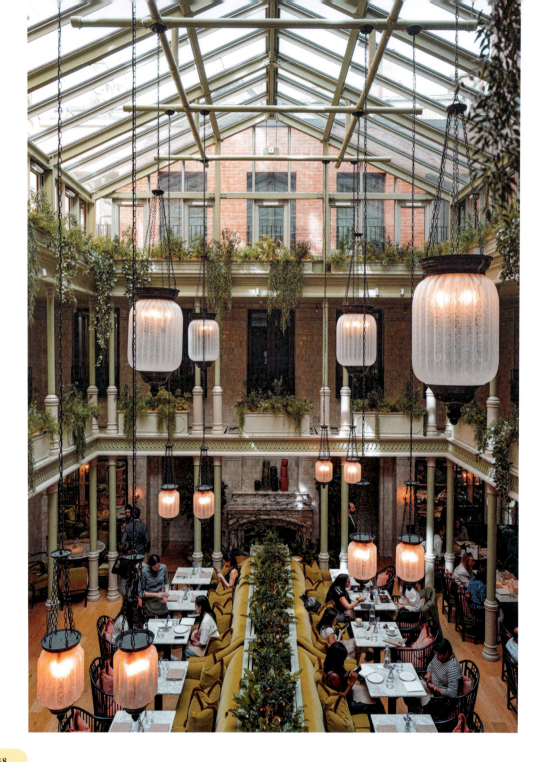

NoMad

BRUNCH INSIDE A GREENHOUSE

⊖ Covent Garden

NoMad London finds its home in the old Bow Street Magistrates' Court, a Grade II-listed building in Covent Garden. It has quite a lot of history to it, including being the site of Oscar Wilde's prosecution!

Like all NoMad hotels, the restaurant is the pièce de résistance. The grand atrium looks more like a lush greenhouse, with its soaring columns and glass ceiling, which give the space so much light and energy. While it is gorgeous for drinks and dinner, we really fancied checking out the weekend brunch offering and we were not disappointed. The avocado on toast with maitake mushrooms and parsley was seriously one of the best we have ever had; it made us feel like we were somewhere in LA (there is something about the avo on toasts there, we promise). We also recommend the NoMad breakfast sandwich with fried Burford egg and cheese. Just delicious.

Peggy Jean

BRUNCH ON A BARGE

⊖ Richmond

This lovingly restored Victorian barge securely anchored in Richmond serves up an Aussie-style brunch which we are sure you'll love as much as we do. With dreamy views across the Thames, Peggy Jean is a crowd-pleaser.

The pastel pink-and-light blue boat was once property of Jesus College Oxford, from its boat-racing days. It now exists purely for our delight as a wonderful al fresco spot. Brunch is available every day until 3 p.m. but bear in mind the summer terraces are on a first-come, first-serve basis.

The Bondi – bacon, poached eggs and mushrooms on charcoal sourdough – is a hit with customers, and the Dirty Daisy, made with poached eggs and crispy tater tots (yummy) really opened our taste buds to all things Sydney-like. But that's not all you can find at Peggy Jean.

Leave some space for its award-winning banana bread, made with delightful whipped mascarpone cream, fresh berries, almonds and honey. When in Rome, right?

+ INSIDER TIP
〰〰〰〰〰〰

Come back in the evening for a summer spritzer or two – to enjoy one of the best sunset spots in town.

Sunday in Brooklyn

PANCAKE MANNA
FROM HEAVEN

Bond Street/Notting Hill Gate

Coming directly from Brooklyn, Sunday in Brooklyn, the Notting Hill and Marylebone incarnations, brought its famous pancakes to the London Brunch scene, and quite frankly we could not be happier that we don't have to catch a red-eye to have a bite of these heavenly sweets.

Perfect any day of the week, and not just on Sundays, this airy all-day modern American restaurant is a great setting in which to catch up with friends over brunch at the weekend. Given the fact that there are limited bookable spots, and it is mainly walk-ins, there is usually a queue stretching down the road and around the corner, but it does move pretty fast.

We recommend ordering one savoury dish each, like the egg sandwich bun, made with scrambled eggs, cheddar and gochujang mayo or the Don Ruben omelette, with mole sauce and mushrooms, and, of course, a round of the pancakes to share. You can choose between one pancake or a stack of up to two or three. Just bear in mind they are quite filling! The luxurious hazelnut maple praline makes it impossible to stop eating, and the melting brown butter is quite literally the cherry on top.

MORNING

Vardo

A CHELSEA STAPLE

⊖ Sloane Square

Chances are, if you have been to Chelsea before, you have come across a circular structure in the middle of Duke of York Square. It is usually packed with people, with loads of seating amid lush greenery. That's Vardo for you.

The brainchild of the same team as Caravan, this Chelsea staple institution presents a menu inspired by the nomadic life of a traveller who crossed the world collecting spices and flavours. A nod to this idea is the restaurant's name, referencing the beautiful wagons that the traveller community used to move around in the 1800s.

The concept of no-boundaries can be also seen in the state-of-the-art stone and glass pavillion, which shows off 360-degree wall to floor windows, which are completely retractable into the floor. A UK first, this is a way to make the space feel more airy and create a fluid indoor–outdoor dining experience.

The brunch menu highlights slow-cooked and plant-based techniques, with a focus on healthy, wholesome food. Dishes include a jalapeño cornbread with fried egg, spinach, curd cheese and chilli butter and baked eggs, with spiced tomato, pepper and a chickpea ragu. Brunch at Vardo is a weekend affair, running from 9 a.m. to 4 p.m.

+ INSIDER TIP
〜〜〜〜〜〜

While this is our preferred location, there are several other Vardos across London. And check out Caravan, too (see page 44), from the same owners.

The Ivy Chelsea Garden

AN INSTA-WORTHY GARDEN RESTAURANT

⊖ Sloane Square

Positioned in trendy King's Road, one of the most appealing streets in London, the Ivy Chelsea Garden is one of the most trustworthy brunch places we can think of. All the Ivys have a similar menu and concept but this one, in the pulsing heart of Chelsea, has a secret selling point in addition to its picture-perfect location.

The Ivy Chelsea Garden has, you guessed it, a lush outdoor garden with cosy firepit. So, if you are looking for a tranquil al fresco dining spot for a long overdue catch-up with friends, this may well be the place for you. During the Chelsea Flower Show, at the end of May, the Ivy Chelsea goes all out with flower decorations – as do many places in Chelsea – but this is something you definitely don't want to miss. Alternatively, wait for Christmas time it puts on a similar show with festive displays and decorations around the door and on the exterior walls. You'll trip over people having their photos taken outside.

On the menu, there is something for everyone to enjoy, whether you are in the mood for a healthier option such as yogurt with granola or a vegan or vegetarian dish. No matter the occasion or the company, chocolate ivy-adorned cappuccinos, and all the classics, such as avocado eggs benny and decadent buttermilk pancakes will be waiting for you here.

+ INSIDER TIP

Open seven days a week, the brunch menu is available from 11 a.m. to 4 p.m. on the weekends only.

Tomtom Coffee House

BELGRAVIA'S PRETTIEST BRUNCH VENUE

🚇 Pimlico/Victoria

Head to Belgravia on a weekend, and chances are you'll spot a pretty substantial queue in front of this popular brunch spot. On a warm day – well, on any day, really – the tables out front are packed with couples and friends enjoying brunch, while sipping on a colourful smoothie, blue latte or flat white.

The food at Tomtom Coffee House is seriously delicious and irresistibly pretty, so no wonder people love this place so much. From the menu, we recommend the super colourful açai bowl, granola and coconut yogurt bowl or the scrumptious pancakes with seasonal fruits and cream cheese. If sweets are not your thing, you'll love the poached eggs and the smashed avo on toast on a bed of kale and feta, or possibly the super green omelette on sourdough is more your thing. Or why not have a toastie, made with Tomtom's signature homemade focaccia? There's so much to choose from.

From autumn specials, such as pumpkin spice or maple lattes, to gingerbread ones in winter, Tomtom is as seasonal as one can be. Even its outdoor installation changes according to the season, with golden leaves in autumn, pretty flowers in the springtime and cosy twinkling lights for the festivities. No matter when you visit, you are in for a treat: it looks beautiful every single time.

Friends of Ours

A TRULY
INTERNATIONAL
BRUNCH
EXPERIENCE

Old Street

Tucked away, down a sun-trapped side street, just off the busy City Road, in the heart of Hoxton, is Friends of Ours – a local brunch spot with scrumptious dishes and great coffee.

It is a walk-in place only, but it has quite a lot of seating space available, especially outside on wooden benches. And fear not, even if it's busy, space will always be found to seat you. As the name suggests, you can expect the friendliest service and such a relaxed atmosphere that you won't want to leave.

Looking at the menu, you'll find traditional brunch items such as eggs on toast – sourdough which they get from Dusty Knuckle, so you'll know you are in for a treat – or a too-pretty-to-eat seasonal French toast (a must-order in our opinion). In addition, and this is why a lot of customers come here, are the globally inspired dishes. These include a çilbir, with Turkish eggs, smoked eggplant and toasted focaccia, or a gochujang sweetheart cabbage on sourdough, with smoked tofu and black garlic. One thing for sure, even if we have been there many times now, Friends of Ours still manages to surprise us, with its ever-changing menu.

MORNING

Coffee Breaks

We all love walking around London but when tiredness threatens to overwhelm us, there is only one thing to do. Sit down and grab a coffee! With so many options around, it can be quite overwhelming to find the right spot that fits the bill, so we have done the hard work for you. Here are a few of our favourites, dotted about the capital.

TERRACE BAR AT TATE MODERN

Perfect for a break in between museum hopping, the Terrace Bar at the Tate Modern boasts stunning views over St Paul's Cathedral and the Thames. Order a coffee and a slice of cake and read a few pages of your book among the bustle.

ITALIAN BEAR CHOCOLATE

Forget coffee, why not indulge in London's most decadent hot chocolate dripping with triple white, milk and dark chocolate. Seriously delicious, you can also add your own twist, including chilli, cinnamon or cardamon. The ganache chocolate cake is a must and if you are feeling brave you can add triple chocolate to that too; we won't judge. During the weekends, bookings are strongly recommended in both the Soho and Fitzrovia branches.

RALPH'S COFFEE

If you need a break in between shopping, sit outside the Ralph Lauren Café, in thriving Bond Street. With the best people-watching, cute coffee cups and irresistible cookies, we absolutely adore it.

WATCHHOUSE

With locations dotted all over London, WatchHouse is a stylish spot for a coffee break and to grab something to eat. Every store is unique and tailored around the local neighbourhood, with Somerset House being our favourite. Grab a chair, join the other Londoners catching a break and sit in the sun with an iced coffee and admire the bankside landscape.

REDEMPTION ROASTERS

The world's first prison-based coffee company, Redemption Roasters aims to reduce reoffending by training and employing convicts to become baristas and coffee roasters, thanks to its behind bars roastery, originally in the young offenders' institute in Aylesbury, as of writing now at HMP The Mount, a category C men's prison. With truly ethical standards, and a mission to rehabilitate, be sustainable and empower female coffee producers, Redemption Roasters not only is doing good but produces truly great coffee. These little coffee shops, which began in Lamb's Conduit Street, are now scattered all around London, so you are never too far from a great cuppa.

BAR ITALIA

Established in 1946 in Soho, this is the Holy Grail for many a London coffee lover – and your spot for coffee the Italian way. With the look of an old-school Italian café and an original Gaggia coffee machine that has been making espressos for over fifty years, Bar Italia stands out from a world of chains and corporate coffee places.

V&A CAFÉ

The world's first museum restaurant, dating from the late 1860s, this opulently designed coffee place is the perfect spot to work away on your laptop or to have a rest, after hours of wandering the fantastic array of art, design and costumes found in the galleries at South Ken's Victoria and Albert Museum. The lighting is amazing, the décor impressive, bringing to mind grand old cafés of the past. And, oh yes, the freshly baked scones are to die for!

AFTERNOON

LUNCH

Apricity

THE MOST SUSTAINABLE RESTAURANT IN LONDON

⊖ Bond Street

Apricity, which means 'the warmth of the sun in winter', is a Michelin Green Star restaurant in Mayfair. Chef-owner Chantelle Nicholson runs a low-waste operation, whether it's the suppliers, how they wash the dishes, the décor or even how the menu is displayed.

British produce is championed, with a seasonal approach, using regeneratively farmed meat and sustainably caught fish from the British Isles. The chairs are made from decommissioned Coke bottles and the walls are bare plaster. It doesn't get more sustainable than Apricity, we can assure you!

The menu features produce at the height of the season from small-scale farmers and producers and from locally foraged goods, which means it constantly changes. The dishes are presented Mayfair-style, with an incredible attention to detail. The London red butterhead lettuce, Kultured miso aioli and crispy peas are assembled into a flower and really is a work of art! The Black Pearl and Oyster mushrooms, hand-dived Firth of Clyde scallops, beef fat and black garlic takoyaki, taramasalata and poached forced Kentish rhubarb, goldencomb and cashew cream are also all very tasty (and pretty), and really worth ordering if they are on the menu when you go.

What about the drinks? There is a long list of British sparklings and whites that champion English vineyards and winemakers. Of course.

AFTERNOON

Campania

A LITTLE BIT OF PASTA AFTER FLOWER SHOPPING

⊖ Bethnal Green/Hoxton

It's Sunday, you have been to the iconic Columbia Road Flower Market and it's buzzing. You're feeling hungry (and rightly so), and you see the prettiest restaurant and wonder if you should walk in. Well, you should.

Campania is an east London gem. Set in a former 1800s dairy, this rustic chic Italian restaurant serves – as the name suggests – dishes from the Campania region in Italy. It almost feels like walking into an Italian home, with nonnas making fresh pasta, as if they were preparing an Italian Sunday feast. The must-order is obviously pasta, and we decided to try the scialatielli lobster and the stracciatella, cime di rapa and acciughe, with a glass of Taurasi from the Campania region. It was wonderful.

+ INSIDER TIP

Book a table outside during the summer and you'll have the best people-watching experience in east London.

The Cinnamon Club

THE MPS FAVOURITE INDIAN RESTAURANT

⊖ St James's Park/Westminster

The Cinnamon Club is like no other Indian restaurant in London. Set in the impressive location of the Grade II-listed former Westminster Library, chef Vivek Singh's restaurant opened in 2001 and has been challenging conceptions of what modern Indian cuisine is ever since. And all this in a room where you are surrounded by high walls covered in classic books.

The Cinnamon Club is a favourite of MPs due to its proximity to the Houses of Parliament, to the extent that there used to be a bell that was rung to summon the MPs back to work after their lunch breaks.

The food is outstanding and we would recommend going for the tasting menu so that you can try a little bit of everything. The dishes are colourful and well-presented, and if you are not used to spicy foods, the serving staff will let you know if something is particularly hot, and offer alternative suggestions. The Cinnamon Club serves equally good vegan, vegetarian, from the sea, from the land and wild options.

+ INSIDER TIP
〰〰〰〰〰

Enjoy the Saturday Jazz Brunch, from 12 to 2:30 p.m. At £45 a head, it's a great and more economical way to taste some of the fine dishes on the menu.

Daphne's

THE BEST FESTIVE
TERRACE IN LONDON

⊖ Sloane Square

+ INSIDER TIP

You can't reserve a table on the terrace at the moment – it's on a first come first served basis, but you can call and ask the lovely staff to leave a note and they will do their best.

A Chelsea establishment, Daphne's is a chic Italian restaurant popular with locals, celebrities and couples. The restaurant opened in the 1960s and since then has served authentic Italian regional dishes. Think spaghetti alle vongole, parmigiana, burrata and cotoletta alla Milanese.

The interior is very elegant and upscale, with vintage Murano chandeliers and European art throughout the restaurants. The best part though, for us, is the hidden terrace, which is beautifully decorated for the Chelsea Flower Show and Christmas.

We particularly love visiting during the festive period and sitting by the cosy fireplace on the terrace, sipping festive cocktails and breathing in the atmosphere.

Pollini

EATING WITH YOUR EYES

🚇 Ladbroke Grove

This Italian restaurant in Notting Hill is a work of art. Pollini is set in Ladbroke Hall, a 120-year-old building that originally served as a car factory, showroom and office for the Sunbeam Talbot Motor Company. In 2019, this space was converted into a cultural hub, with art displayed throughout the whole building. The restaurant, which is inside the grand lobby, blends perfectly with its surroundings, with artwork throughout, which the manager happy to talk you through.

Chef Pollini's dishes are inspired by the days when he used to help his grandmother in the kitchen, and you can savour the Italian flavours below a majestic chandelier designed by Nacho Carbonell. Vaniglia al momento was probably our favourite dish, which is an organic Madagascan vanilla bean gelato freshly made for the table. There's also a bambino menu available for little hands.

+ INSIDER TIP

If you are into live music as much as we are, they also have fantastic Friday jazz nights.

Frederick's

AN ISLINGTON INSTITUTION

⊖ Angel

Frederick's is an Islington classic. Family run since 1969 by the Segal family, this restaurant is the kind of place you go to with your family for a Sunday lunch or with friends for a catch-up after a browse in Camden Passage's antique shops. The interiors are spacious and airy, with old-school art, and there is a pretty hidden garden in the back that you would only really know about if you're a local.

As for the menu, it's as relaxed as the vibe of the restaurant. The European-inspired dishes include Frederick's gazpacho with basil sorbet, pan-fried scallops, beef carpaccio and English asparagus, while for seafood lovers as a main there is the pistachio-crusted rare tuna, pan-fried halibut and miso black cod. As for meat, the chateaubriand, Welsh lamb chop and the breaded organic chicken escalope should do the trick.

Finish in style with a delicious chocolate fondant with pistachio ice cream, a salted caramel panna cotta or a white chocolate cheesecake with raspberry sorbet.

Flour & Grape

A QUEUE WORTH DOING

⊖ Bermondsey

+ INSIDER TIP
〰〰〰〰〰
While you can't book, the Dojo app makes it easier to dine here.

If you have ever walked to the end of Bermondsey, you will have surely noticed one thing: a line of people queuing for Flour & Grape. What is it about this Italian restaurant that makes it so special? Well, a few things really.

The first thing you will see while queuing is a lady making fresh pasta at the window, always a good sign! The pasta is indeed fresh, absolutely delicious and reasonably priced. As is the wine, meaning you won't break the bank if you want a bottle of Primitivo or even Nebbiolo with your meal. The sharing starters are also excellent, with the burrata really standing out – probably the best we have had in London.

Our favourite pasta dishes are the casarecce 'arrabiata', the bucatini cacio e pepe and the tortelloni, but to be honest anything we have eaten there has been excellent.

So if you are still wondering, yes, it is worth the queue.

AFTERNOON

Jamavar

INDIAN FINE DINING
AT ITS BEST

⊖ Bond Street

Michelin-starred Jamavar serves seriously delicious, fine-dining Indian food in Mayfair. It has become our go-to over the years when we fancy a more sophisticated, light and balanced Indian meal in the city.

The interiors are smartly done, the restaurant looking like a colonial-style gentleman's club, with dark panelled wood and beautiful walls adorned with Indian art. The menu explores all regions of India, with both homestyle regional dishes and ones you would find only in royal kitchens. We would definitely recommend going for the tasting menu, which takes you on a full journey of India without leaving Mayfair.

What is truly special for us, though, is the Alphonso Mango menu that runs through May. To celebrate this special fruit, Jamavar adorns the outside terrace with all things mango. Every dish on the menu features mangos to some extent, with things like mango lassi made from Alphonso mangoes and yogurt, scallop mangai, made with mango chilli salsa, coconut cream and roasted southern Indian spices, kairee jheenga, made with southern-spiced prawns, chilli, coriander and mango pachadi, and the most delicious mango-based dessert, which changes every year.

Morito

DELICIOUS SHARING PLATES IN HACKNEY

 Hoxton

Morito on Hackney Road is one of our favourite restaurants in east London. It's one of those places that springs to mind when deciding where to go with friends to enjoy delicious small plates, with a good fun vibe, without breaking the bank.

The menu at Morito draws influences from southern Spain, North Africa and the eastern Mediterranean, with a Cretan twist added by head chef Marianna Leivaditaki, who grew up and worked in her family's fish restaurant on the Greek island.

The tapas and mezze-style plates are made to share, with dishes such as cheese fritters with Cretan thyme honey, fried aubergine drizzled with date molasses and topped with feta cheese, chargrilled lamb chops covered in anchovy butter and Cretan sausage, flatbread, guindilla and yoghurt.

The wine list is very reasonably priced, with interesting choices and even a few orange wines, if that's your bag, by the glass.

+ INSIDER TIP
〰〰〰〰〰

There is a smaller, sister branch situated on Exmouth Market, which is great for people-watching.

Bellanger

SOUTHERN FRENCH
CUISINE IN ISLINGTON

 Angel

Bellanger is a local favourite restaurant in Angel, right next door to Noci (see page 194). Southern French-inspired, it is styled with the elegance of Europe's Grand cafés, with high ceilings, classic red leather brasserie seating, wood panelling and artwork all over the walls. And as with every good brasserie, it has a large terrace for people-watching and Apéro.

It's the perfect spot for anything, really. Being part of the Wolseley Hospitality group, it excels in breakfast and brunch, but our favourite time to visit is for lunch on the terrace during summer. The menu includes bistro favourites like steak tartare, escargots and Provençal goat's cheese salad, and seasonal dishes like stuffed courgette flowers and the pan-seared sea bream with couscous.

+ INSIDER TIP
〰〰〰〰〰

At dinnertime, it's the perfect spot for an intimate date, and there is live music on Wednesdays and Thursdays.

JOIA

THE BEST VIEWS OVER BATTERSEA POWER STATION

⊖ Battersea Power Station

When Battersea Power Station completed its renovation in 2022, one of the first things we thought about was how amazing it would be to have a rooftop restaurant with power station view. The art'otel took care of that.

JOIA – meaning 'jewel' in Portuguese – is the first UK restaurant of two Michelin-starred chef Henrique Sá Pessoa, who, influenced by the rich flavours of Catalonia and Portugal, has put together a delicious unfussy sharing plate menu with British-sourced ingredients. The pastel pink and green interiors are elegant and serene, with potted plants that add that Mediterranean feel. The floor-to-ceiling windows have striking views of the infamous chimneys and rooftops of southwest London.

The food is very tasty, and you can expect dishes such as classic tortilla with aioli, salt cod tortilla, Iberico ham croquettes, Carabineros prawns with orzo and bisque, and bacalhau a bras. The desserts may be the main contender here though, with Basque cheesecake and arroz de leche, both absolutely to die for.

+ INSIDER TIP
〰〰〰〰〰

If you head to JOIA during summer, there is also a superb rooftop on the sixteenth floor, which serves some of chef Henrique's favourite dishes and refreshing summer cocktails.

A
F
T
E
R
N
O
O
N

Luca

HOMEMADE PASTA
IN CLERKENWELL

◉ Farringdon

Luca is the type of Italian restaurant you recommend to a friend when you don't want to go wrong. It may be the rustic interior, the covered garden that reminds us of a Roman giardino or the pasta, which is all made in-house, that make this restaurant so special.

Luca is the sister restaurant of the acclaimed Clove Club in Shoreditch and has the peculiarity of being – as they say so themselves – Britalian. That means that they cook Italian recipes without Italian ingredients, and almost exclusively with ingredients sourced in the UK. That doesn't mean that the dishes are less tasty than if you were having them in a trattoria in Tuscany's rolling hills.

Our favourite dishes are the Parmesan fries (you won't believe how light they are until you try them), the homemade truffle agnolotti and the tiramisu. All to enjoy with a glass of Barolo.

Maggie Jones's

A PLACE FOR A
COSY LUNCH DATE

⊖ High Street Kensington

Walking into Maggie Jones's feels like
walking into a Cotswolds farmhouse
rather than bustling High Street Ken.
Think baskets with dry lavender, tin
watering cans and saddles hanging from
the ceilings, mismatching chairs and
tables, cupboards full of crockery and
candles on every table.

Maggie Jones's opened in 1963 as Nan's
Kitchen. It was very popular with locals
and soon became Princess Margaret and
Lord Snowdon's favourite restaurant, where
she would book under the name 'Maggie
Jones' and hide in one of its secluded
booths. To honour this connection, the
restaurant changed its name in the 1970s,
and we love it.

As per the menu, Maggie's has been
cooking traditional home-cooked British
food since its opening. Expect to see
on your candlelit tables dishes such as
sausage and mash, hearty stews, fish
pies, Stilton mousse, roasted guinea fowl
in white wine sauce and grilled salmon.
It also serves the most delicious Sunday
roast, but do book well in advance as it is
very popular with locals. As for desserts,
the bread and butter pudding and apple
crumble are our favourites.

Mimi Mei Fair

CHINESE FOOD MAYFAIR-STYLE

⊖ Green Park

Tucked away on a quiet street in Mayfair in a three-storey Georgian townhouse, Mimi Mai Fair, by talented restaurateur Samyukta Nair, takes you on a culinary journey through China and Singapore.

Samyukta imagined the space as the residence of Empress Mimi, keeper of the most sacred Chinese culinary secrets. The décor takes inspiration from late nineteenth-century and early twentieth-century Chinese decorative styles, while the menu is meant to share, with dishes such as crispy golden langoustines and périgord truffle, Peking duck bao, a selection of dim sum, Singapore chilli prawns and Australian abalone. But what really steals the show is the apple wood-fired roasted Peking duck, which is served and cut at the table and creates the perfect Insta-moment.

Even though there is a Mayfair-style wine list, we generally order the cocktails, which are very well presented and tasty, particularly the Smoked Banana Old Fashioned and the Mimi-tini.

Lisboeta

A FOODIE LOVE
LETTER TO LISBON

🚇 Goodge Street/
Tottenham Court Road

+ INSIDER TIP
〜〜〜〜

*Try the menu do día, two courses
for £35, available Tuesday to Friday,
12–2:30 p.m.*

Lisboeta describes itself as a love letter to Lisbon, and we really couldn't agree more. If you are looking for a taste of sunny Portugal on one of those many rainy days we seem to get, chef Nuno Mendez's dishes will definitely do the trick.

The restaurant is set across three floors of a colourful townhouse on Charlotte Street, and diners can choose to sit either at the impressive limestone counter next to the open kitchen on the ground floor or in the art-covered upstairs dining space. The atmosphere is fun and vibrant, making for the perfect spot to lunch and catch up with friends.

As for the food, the dishes take inspiration from Mendez's hometown flavours, with a mix of both non-traditional petiscos, or small plates, together with tasca-style larger sharing plates. We particularly loved the arroz de Marisco, one of its signature dishes, the bolo de bolacha, a biscuit cake with coffee and ice cream, and the pão de ló olive oil cake. You will want to order some wine, as Lisboeta has one of the biggest Portuguese wine selections in London. Absolutely to die for.

Ognisko

CLASSY POLISH RESTAURANT

⊖ South Kensington

On Exhibition Road in South Kensington, a step away from the Natural History and the Victoria and Albert museums, lies, arguably, London's best Polish restaurant, Ognisko.

Set in a magnificent Victorian townhouse, which has been home to the Polish Hearth Club since the Second World War, this restaurant is the centre of social and cultural life for London's Polish community. The high-ceiling, ornate dining room is stunning. The ingredients remain humble though, with traditional Polish dishes throughout the menu. Think barszcz, which is clear beetroot soup with mushroom, pasztecik, pierogi filled with cheese, potato and onion, and kopytka dumplings sautéed with chestnuts and forest mushrooms. Ah, and don't forget a shot of vodka or two during your meal, recommended by the very friendly Polish staff.

Our favourite feature, though, is probably the outdoor terrace, which overlooks a small private park away from London's hustle and bustle. It's very spacious, making it the perfect spot for an extended family Sunday lunch or lunch with friends.

+ INSIDER TIP
〰〰〰〰

If you're of Polish nationality or descent, pop into nearby Ognisko Polski (the Polish Hearth), one of oldest UK's Polish members' clubs. It holds cultural events, including the Kino Club, a film series with a Polish actor or director in attendance, discussing their work.

Stanley's

LUNCH IN A
SECRET GARDEN
IN CHELSEA
LOCATED JUST OFF
THE KING'S ROAD

Sloane Square/
South Kensington

Stanley's is one of those places that only locals know about. The crowd is very Chelsea, with friends gossiping over lunch and well-dressed ladies discussing the latest fashion trends with their pooches.

The courtyard is designed to look like a quintessentially British garden and is equipped with heaters for those not-so-sunny London days. Former MasterChef contestant Olivia Burt's dishes are made with British ingredients and feature cured pork tenderloin and piccalilli, burrata with courgette, mint and seeds and pork and nduja croquettes to start, with roasted cod, dry-aged sirloin and whole gilthead bream as mains.

But the truth here is in the pudding. The menu changes with the seasons, but when we last visited the sticky toffee pudding and the orange cream and the chiffon cake, rhubarb and bay custard were to die for.

Studio Frantzén

NORDIC DESIGN AND JAPANESE PRECISION

⊖ Knightsbridge

Over recent years, Harrods has become more and more a foodie's destination, in addition to being one of the best department stores in the world. The Food Hall, always a foodie destination, is what dreams are made of, and you can also indulge in afternoon tea in the Tea Rooms, or even sushi, ramen, pasta, pizza or more in the Dining Hall after a day of intense shopping.

Our favourite eatery, though, is on the fifth and sixth floors, and is the East Asian-influenced Nordic restaurant Studio Frantzén, opened by the famous Swedish chef Björn Frantzén. The restaurant's interiors are elegant and minimalist, while the menu blends Nordic and Asian cuisines, serving dishes such as roasted scallops with scrambled duck eggs, tartare of tuna and red deer, and herring caviar and dirty seaweed oil. We would also recommend the warm laminated milk bread à la croissant with blond miso butter and borage honey. It's absolutely to die for.

+ INSIDER TIP
〰〰〰〰〰

Studio Frantzén also features Harrods's only rooftop terrace, which is a great spot for pre-dinner drinks, with views over Knightsbridge.

The Summerhouse

FRESH SEAFOOD ON THE CANALS

⊖ Maida Vale/Warwick Avenue

Walking along the Grand Union Canal towards Little Venice can be one of the most charming things to do during the summer months in London. Ah, the narrowboats, the swans, the leafy trees. It's just so idyllic, isn't it? The only challenge sometimes is to find the perfect place to eat that matches this vibe. We think we know such a place.

The Summerhouse is a stunning seasonal fish restaurant just along the banks of the canal, the perfect spot to relax and watch life go by while feasting on fresh seafood, oysters and summer salads.

The interiors almost give you the feeling of being on holiday, and the menu features dishes such as asparagus with egg beignet, black garlic aioli, Parma ham crisp, seared scallops, burrata and the 'super healthy salad' to start, while for mains you will be spoilt for choice, with whole baked sea bass, risotto primavera, sea trout and, of course, the catch of the day. There is a great selection of gins for your G&T and some lovely whites by the glass. Almost like being in South of France, right?

The desserts are also very refreshing, with dishes such as coconut and mango rice pudding, Eton Mess and knickerbocker glory on the menu.

Taverna Trastevere

SIMPLE DELICIOUS
ROMAN CUISINE

⊖ Clapham Junction

If it's one of those miserable rainy days in London and you want to be virtually transported to Rome for a few hours, Taverna Trastevere is the closest you can get. This restaurant in Clapham Junction delivers authentic Roman cuisine to your table. It's as simple as that.

The interiors are rustic and the restaurant is styled just like an osteria would be styled in Rome's iconic Trastevere neighbourhood, and there are also a few tables outside for sunnier days. The dishes on the menu are what you would expect. Spaghetti alla carbonara, saltimbocca alla romana, cacio e pepe, artichokes, with classic Italian drinks like Negroni, Aperol spritz and prosecco.

Taverna Trastevere is simplicity at its best, which characterises Roman cuisine, and we absolutely love it.

Trullo

A PROPER NEIGHBOURHOOD ITALIAN

⊖ Highbury & Islington

Trullo isn't on some trendy, fancy or hipster street. It's a proper neighbourhood trattoria in Islington, just by Highbury & Islington Tube station. It's not a restaurant you stumble upon; it's a restaurant you know about.

Trullo is packed mostly with locals and the occasional Arsenal fan on match days. It offers very simple, seasonal food, with, of course, homemade pasta. The Italian-inspired menu is printed every day, as the dishes really depend on what produce the team finds fresh in the market. So you may never eat the same plate of pasta twice!

The interior is very rustic, virtually transporting you to Tuscany, and the open kitchen really contributes to the vibrant scene. It's split over two floors, but we would definitely recommend booking upstairs for lunch as it's bright and airy, and downstairs for dinner as it's moodier.

The Water House Project

A HOME AWAY FROM HOME

⊖ Bethnal Green

This restaurant in Bethnal Green, just by
the Regent's Canal, really is like no other in
London. The concept of The Water House
Project is 'social fine dining'; that is delicious
small plates in a convivial atmosphere.
Before opening the restaurant, chef Gabriel
Waterhouse had been running supper clubs
in his home, and you can really tell by how
welcoming the atmosphere is when you arrive.

The Water House Project only serves tasting
menus and does one seating per day, with a
ten-course evening menu or seven-course
Saturday lunch menu that changes every three
months. Most of the vegetables are sourced
from the outskirts of London, the meat from
the Lake District and the fish from the south of
England. The low-intervention wines are from
small producers – as you would expect – and
really complement the food.

The Nordic-style design is cleverly done, so
that you feel as if you are a guest in someone's
home, with the friendly chefs cooking in front
of your eyes and serving the food to your table.
The dishes are everchanging but expect to see
Orkney scallops, Yorkshire rhubarb, London
honey and Cornish pollock.

Mount Street
Restaurant

A MASTERPIECE
IN MAYFAIR

Bond Street/Hyde Park Corner

Set above The Audley Public House (see page 124), this restaurant in Mayfair is a work of art. Literally. Think dining surrounded by a backdrop of £50 million worth of fine art, by the likes of Matisse, Lucian Freud, Warhol, Louise Bourgeois and Picasso, to mention a few. Even the floor is an artwork in itself. *The Broken Floor* by Rashid Johnson is a floor made up of varying mosaics throughout the restaurant.

The food is equally impressive. The chefs work closely with local farmers and growers, with the beef and lamb arriving straight from their farm in Somerset. Starters include mock turtle croquettes, English asparagus cooked in seaweed butter, Orkney scallops and, our favourite, the Omelette Arnold Bennett, beautifully served and packed with delicious haddock. The main event is probably the lobster pie for two, which comes with the head plonked in the middle and is plated at the table.

Mount Street Restaurant also has four stunning private rooms, all styled differently from one another, perfect for any special occasion, but they don't come cheap, as you can imagine!

Brixton Village

⊖ Brixton

If you have ever stepped foot in Brixton, in south London, you will know it has its own vibe: the sounds, the smells, the food, the people, everything seems different. Today, a thriving global community, Brixton historically became a popular area for the Afro-Caribbean communities, particularly people from Jamaica, post-Windrush, to settle in. By the 1960s, it had become one of the UK's largest areas of Caribbean settlement.

These Caribbeans, from Jamaica, Guyana, Grenada, St Lucia, Trinidad and Tobago, and more, brought with them their own culture, music and cuisine, and the area became a popular place for people to buy West Indian and Asian produce. Alongside this, street food stalls and restaurants opened, using ingredients such as yams and plantains alongside more traditionally and easily sourced British and European ingredients, and Brixton market became the place to go to for West Indian and African produce in London. Over the decades, the area has gone through deprivation and wealth, becoming a place of regeneration, and Brixton Village, as the market's known, became a Grade II-listed area in 2010, reflecting its importance to Black history and the community in the post-war period.

Fast forward to 2024, and you'll see that this bustling covered food market is strongly influenced by the area's migrant roots, with some of the most sought-after Jamaican, Colombian, Ethiopian and Brazilian restaurants, as well as cocktail bars, specialist coffee shops and much more.

Walking through the market is an experience itself, with locals buying fruit and vegetables, fish and meat, and a generally younger crowd curious to try new cuisines at very affordable prices. It can be quite overwhelming and difficult to choose where to dine, so here are a few favourites.

If you are looking for authentic Caribbean dishes, head to Etta's Seafood Kitchen, set up by local resident and 'original Brixtonian' Etta, and for Caribbean dishes with a twist, to Danclair's. For African dishes, Light of Africa is a must and offers vegetarian and vegan Ethiopian and Eritrean food, made with spices imported from the former. Expect traditional injera and local Ethiopian beer on tap. For Colombian food and seriously delicious arepas de queso, head to Santaferino and find live music, large portions and very warm hospitality. To finish, head to Brazilian Reem's for traditional brigadeiros, a dessert made with condensed and evaporated milk and chocolate.

AFTERNOON

STREET
FOOD

Maltby Street Market

FOR IN-THE-KNOW FOODIES

 Bermondsey

Maltby Street Market is the weekend only 'secret in the city' street food market located in the Ropewalk in Bermondsey. This little alley is big in personality, adorned with many colourful flags and lined with Victorian railway arches. The smells, sounds and vibrant atmosphere will capture your heart – and stomach.

This is the place where many traders start out on their food dream journeys before moving on to opening shops and bigger ventures. It serves as a foodie incubator. A true paradise for savvy foodies and those in the know, Maltby Street Market is really a test ground for new ideas, street food fusions and novelty items. Almost totally unadvertised, the market is always packed, so it's best to go early!

The more permanent sit-down eateries are nestled within the railway arches, while the stalls operate on a gentle rotation so that there is always something new to enjoy. The incredible moussaka from the Greek Pot, the cheesy mooncheese toasties and la criolla empanadas are some we really can't live without.

AFTERNOON

87

Borough Market

THE OLDEST FOOD MARKET IN LONDON

⊖ London Bridge

Borough Market, near London Bridge in Southwark, is true heaven for foodies and definitely an unmissable stop when visiting the capital. Active for more than one thousand years, Borough Market is the oldest food market in London, yet excluding its beautiful, historic architecture and heritage, there is nothing 'old' about this place.

Borough Market is fashionable, dynamic and an ever-changing melting pot of international cuisines. Given the freshness of its produce – food stalls vie with eateries – it's no coincidence that many London chefs come to shop here for their restaurants. Be prepared to find unusual foods that you probably won't be able to find easily elsewhere in London, whether it's sugarcane juices, meats from South Tyrol or spicy sauces from Calabria in Italy. Borough Market certainly knows how to keep up with food trends.

From the viral chocolate-covered strawberries to raclette with potatoes and melting cheese sandwiches from Kappacasein, you'll be spoilt for choice. An international cuisine heaven, it's easy to travel with your taste buds alone. Try Horn OK Please, for some of the best vegetarian Indian street food, Shuck for fluffy Israeli pitas or Porteña for Argentinian empanadas.

There are so many places to try, it's seriously impossible to list them all. Once your stomach is satisfied, continue your day in the area and proceed for a walk along the South Bank. Don't forget to grab an ice cream from Gelateria 3BIS and walk towards the Tate Modern, passing by the Globe Theatre and arriving at the Millennium Bridge, where you can view the historic magnificence of St Paul's. Once you have reached the London Eye, we won't judge you if you head back again for another round of foodie exploration, with a stop possibly for a cuppa at the Tate Modern Terrace Bar (see page 89) along the way.

A
F
T
E
R
N
O
O
N

Old Spitalfields Market

THE ORIGINAL EAST LONDON MARKET

Ⓔ Liverpool Street

Old Spitalfields Market, the famous covered market in east London, is an unmissable foodie stop for tourists and Londoners alike. Small producers, local craft people, independent vintage stores, food stalls and even a handful of selected well-known boutiques all live under the same roof.

The market was originally built in 1876, and its architecture is one of the most amazing examples of Victorian market halls still in use. Today the market floor is brimming with unique food stalls and restaurants. It's right here, in the heart of the market that you'll find the Kitchens, a handpicked collection of chefs who and restaurants which create an all-day street food experience.

An exciting destination of international cuisines, old-school street food and contemporary creations allows us to experience all kind of flavours and different cultures. Not to be missed are the Insta-famous sandwiches at Crunch, made with a crispy toasted golden brioche and filled with the likes of umami-fried mushrooms, truffle beef patties or southern-fried chicken cutlets.

Look out for the Pleasant Lady, serving jian bing – a filled savoury crêpe which is China's favourite street food dish. The Dumpling Shack always offers amazing dumplings and attracts the biggest crowd of hungry Londoners in the whole market. It is famous for its signature shenhjianbao – soup dumplings from Shanghai. Head to Ricebrother to try its sweet and savoury rice roll 'burritos'. For a sweet treat grab a fluffy pancake, filled with interesting flavours such as adzuki bean, Matcha or vanilla custard from the Wheelcake Island.

Open seven days a week, it is best to visit on a weekday, after the lunchtime rush, if you want to avoid the crowds and find a nice little spot to sit down and enjoy your food.

Sud Italia

PIZZA A PORTAFOGLIO ON WHEELS

⊖ Liverpool Street

Sud Italia, set in Spitalfields Market, is home to an iconic street food from Naples – the pizza a portafoglio. Still not very well-known abroad, the 'wallet pizza', as it translates in English, is a smaller size, folded twice and wrapped in a sheet of oven paper. Sud Italia was a pioneer in bringing this carb-goodness to London and it has been so well received that the pizza, served from one of the signature vans, can now be seen in Hammersmith and Camden.

The price point is purposely maintained low; just how it would be on the streets of Naples. The wood-fired pizza comes straight from the oven in the iconic Sud Italia's Citroën light blue van, brought by founder Silvestro directly from France. The dough is rigorously made using 00 Napoletana and wholewheat flour, and left to rise for between twenty-four and forty-eight hours, making the pizza very digestible. Ingredients are a big thing and all the mozzarellas get delivered directly from Italy at least twice a week.

+ INSIDER TIP
〰〰〰〰

Grab a smoking hot pizza a portafoglio and eat it with your hands. It's the only way!

Netil Market

A HIDDEN EAST LONDON FOOD MARKET

⊖ Hackney Central

Netil Market is a true hidden gem. Located just off Broadway Market, in east London, it provides a much welcome escape from the crowds. With an industrial, low-key and modern vibe, this destination is certainly different from all its peers. Brought to life by the local creative community from Netil House, with the intent of giving an outlet to local designers, the market has become quite the name for being a foodie destination.

A number of vendors set up in converted shipping containers, such as a barbers, a bike mechanic (how east London!) and a vintage glasses shop. Every Saturday, though, the market comes to life and a number of stalls selling vintage furniture, clothes and artisanal crafts set up for the day, attracting a diverse crowd of shoppers, hipsters, families and foodies.

Foodwise, you'll find a collection of carefully curated stalls, including the popular Sen Noodles or Willy's Pies, which makes homemade hand-pressed proper pies with a dollop of delicious mash. Alternatively, you can grab a slice from the World Famous Gordos, perfect to be enjoyed with a craft beer from the market and eat on the sunny benches, serenaded by Netil Radio. Worth saving some space for is Paulie's Bagels' melted cheese and egg bagel. Just like they do it across the pond. The best time to visit is from Friday to Sunday (9 a.m.–10 p.m.) when all traders are open.

Fine Food Market

A GASTRONOMIC HAVEN IN FORMER ARMY BARRACKS

Sloane Square

Held every Saturday from 10 a.m. until 4 p.m. in the patch of grass adjacent to Duke of York Square, this elegant farmers, market showcases wonderful artisanal produce and food stalls. Curated by the next-door Partridges, the iconic British grocer, it's no wonder the market is so fancy. A long-lasting tradition for Chelsea residents, the market was started in 2005 with the aim of celebrating independent producers, British and international foods and farmers' produce.

Our favourite stallholders include the French crêpes, the Pierogi Company for handmade filled dumplings and, of course, the Maldon Oyster Company.

Our top tip is to bring a picnic blanket with you, as you'll want to join everybody else and sit on the grass on a nice sunny day, with a couple of oysters and a glass of English sparkling wine, of course.

The Mayfair Chippy

SAVOUR POSH FISH
AND CHIPS IN A
CENTRAL LONDON
LOCALE

Bond Street/Marble Arch

Are you looking for a fancy fish and chips? Well, the Mayfair Chippy is the place for you. Set just minutes away from Oxford Street and Hyde Park, this little place has been awarded a 1AA Rosette accreditation since it opened in 2015. The inviting restaurant offers lip-smacking fish and chips alongside an extensive menu of oysters, lobster mac and cheese, crab burgers or a simple grilled 'catch of the day' for a healthier option. But that's not all – the Mayfair Classic is available, vegetarian or vegan with delicious halloumi or to-fish (a vegan fish alternative).

There is truly something for everyone, so you can visit even if your dining companions are not in the mood for fish and chips. The design of the place pays homage to the old-school chippies, with the black and white flooring, vintage sea-themed artwork and panelled walls. In the event of good weather, sit outside with a nice glass of white wine and a few Maldon Rock oysters, before digging into your upmarket fish supper.

La Crêperie de Hampstead

LONDON'S BEST CRÊPES

⊖ Hampstead Heath

This small stall just off Hampstead High Street has gained quite the reputation for serving the best authentic French crêpes in town. It has served Londoners and visitors alike since 1977 and every day of the week attracts crowds of hungry people, tempted by the great reviews and irresistible aromas emanating from this eaterie. Even Ariana Grande took a break from filming to grab a crêpe here!

And they are perfect crêpes, in our opinion. We have no idea what the secret is, but it must be something in the batter, surely? The perfect mix is crisped to perfection by the expert staff (rigorously French and well trained) on the sizzling iron, with a dollop of butter, resulting in flawless crêpes. Whether you have a sweet tooth or savoury, you can find a mouthwatering selection of crêpes and galettes. Or you can be brave and ask for your own creation! Sometimes the staff are not so eager to do this, but, hey, we don't go there for the friendliness.

If you are a savoury person, then there is a classic ham and cheese option, as well as mushroom, tarragon and cheese or ratatouille and cheese. The sweet crêpes are seriously dreamy, with milk, dark or white Belgian chocolate as their signature. On our list to try are the almond maple cream, soaked in real maple syrup, the crème de marrons, with purée of sweetened glacé and chestnuts, and their most popular creation, the Cream Dream, which is made with banana, butter and cream, all topped with peanuts and soaked in maple syrup. It has been on the menu for over twenty-six years, so we think they may possibly be on to something!

Dal Fiorentino

ITALIAN SCHIACCIATA IN HOXTON

⊖ Old Street

Coming directly from Florence, Dal Fiorentino has developed quite the cult in recent years, following videos that went viral on social media. Its unique selling point is Florentine schiacciata, an Italian flatbread, similar to focaccia, born in Tuscany and filled with fresh and traditional ingredients. The high-quality products used at Dal Fiorentino, such as stracciatella cheese, Parma ham and homemade ingredients, such as grilled vegetables and fresh pesto, are all created using authentic recipes to bring delicious street food to the masses.

With evocative names such as Dante, Botticelli and Virgilio, these golden sandwiches are a taste of Italy in every bite! Some of the most popular ones are the Michelangelo, with ribbons of prosciutto, rocket, truffle cream and stracciatella cheese, or La Divina Commedia, with Tuscan Pancetta, gorgonzola and truffle honey. There are many veggie options too – our favourite is I Medici, filled with oozy stracciatella cheese, grilled aubergines and yummy sun-dried tomatoes. Don't miss out on the sweet versions, made with a spread of Nutella or pistachio cream slapped between two pieces of bread. Located in Hoxton, be prepared to queue at peak times to satisfy your Florentine food cravings.

Buon appetito!

Rock & Sole Plaice

LONDON'S OLDEST FISH AND CHIP RESTAURANT

⊖ Covent Garden

Rock & Sole Plaice is a testament and living tribute to our city's culinary history. Established in 1871 as the third ever fish and chips shop, Rock & Sole started serving Covent Garden market and factory workers this lip-smacking delight. Not only did the shop survive the Second World War – it was badly damaged by a bomb blast nearby – but it served as a crucial meeting place for volunteers to discuss food provisions for Londoners who'd lost their homes in the Blitz.

The current name, Rock & Sole Plaice, was given to the shop by two local lads who bought the store in 1974, and it was kept by the family who bought it from them. People visiting from all over the world come to this little shop to try the famous fish and chips, still made using the over 140-year-old traditional recipes passed on to the owners by Rachael and Anna Fenner, whose father, Ray, ran the shop for more than forty years, from the 1920s, and Mary Goody, who'd worked in the shop in the early twentieth century.

+ INSIDER TIP
〰〰〰

If you're not a fish person, try one of the pies available on the menu.

Poppies Fish and Chips

THE ORIGINAL BRITISH STREET FOOD

⊖ Liverpool Street for the original Spitalfields venue

Nothing says street food in Britain like a good old fish and chips. Loved by the whole nation and sought after by all tourists, in towns and on the coast, this fried delight makes everyone happy. And, one question we get asked most is where to go for a good fish and chips in London. And that's equalled by: but what's the absolute best one? While it might be hard to answer the question, we know for certain that Poppies is up among them.

The original Poppies opened in Spitalfields in 1952, and despite further locations in Camden, Portobello and Soho, this establishment is still serving fish and chips the traditional way. Sourcing the freshest catch of the day, the fish is cooked rigorously in high-quality groundnut oil and according to the traditional recipes of Pop, the original owner, the secret behind Poppies' long-lasting success. The result is a crisp, golden batter on the outside with a melt-in-your-mouth flaky, succulent flesh. All fish suppers are served with chips and homemade tartare sauce. The chips are fluffy yet crispy and salty and once you try one it's seriously impossible to stop. Whether eating in or takeaway, people flock to these retro diners for a nostalgic feel and a reminder of that good old Cockney charm that has enthralled Londoners for generations.

Paul Rothe & Son

IRRESISTIBLE CHARM AND CUSTOM-MADE SANDWICHES

⊖ Bond Street

Paul Rothe & Son delicatessen and café in Marylebone, is one of the most unique delis in London. Established in 1900 when the original Paul Rothe came over from Germany, this family owned delicatessen has been passed on by four generations now.

Beautifully stacked pantry staples can be seen inside the irresistibly quaint shop - jams, honey and sauces, along with some worldwide gourmet provisions. We love joining the queue of office workers to grab one of their homemade sandwiches for a takeaway lunch. Paul and Stephen, his son, will greet you with their traditional white coat on and a warm smile combined with looks of concentration as they deal effortlessly with the crowds of people flocking here to get their lunchtime sandwiches.

Of course, one of the reasons people love this place so much is that you can see the sandwiches being made right in front of you, and you can literally pick and mix whatever combination you want to create your custom-made sandwich. Be decisive though or people behind you might start looking at you funny. White or brown bread are some of the choices you'll have to make alongside the fillings of course. Coronation chicken, ham cheese and piccalilli, and pastrami sandwiches are some of customer's favourites. You know, typical British stuff.

The Pie Hole

TAKEAWAY
HANDCRAFTED
PIES IN A LUXURIOUS
LONDON HOTEL

Holborn

Head towards the magnificent Rosewood Hotel, walk past the iconic Pie Room at Holborn Dining Room and chances are you still won't see the Pie Hole. Now, look closely and you'll see a beautiful door. Let yourself get lured closer by the wonderful smell of baked goodies and find the tiny streetside service window. There you are, you've found it! Behind the copper hatch a couple of pastry chefs will be expertly crafting one of Britain's most iconic dishes in a unified and orchestrated way. The menu includes classic chicken and pork pies or dauphinoise potato pie and cheese for a veggie option. Not only do they look beautiful, with their shiny and intricate crusts, but they taste so good! The Pie Hole bakes around two hundred pies per day, so they sure know how to get them right. Practise, as they say, makes perfect.

Humble Crumble

THE WORLD'S FIRST CRUMBLE BAKERY

⊖ Liverpool Street

When you think of street food, probably the oh-so-humble and British crumble doesn't get a look in. A modern take on Britain's most nostalgic dessert, these scrumptious sweet treats take crumble to a new level. Humble Crumble, founded by head baker Kim Innes, came from the idea of warming up customers on a dreary day with comfort food, in the same way that ice cream refreshes and makes people joyful on a sunny day. We are in Britain after all; it rains a lot and everybody loves crumble.

Humble Crumble was set up to be an instant success, and after an incredible world of mouth response and positive reviews, they now have stores in Old Spitalfields Market, Borough Market and Camden Market. But what's inside, you may ask? Is it really the humble English crumble? Each pastel pink cup comes with your choice of fruit as a base, Humble Crumble's signature twice-baked crunchy crumble and a generous dose of Kim's special vanilla custard cream.

You can also add fun toppings, such as blow-torched marshmallows, ice cream or rose petals, and try many different combinations. All crumbles can be made vegan and gluten free too. The Easter, autumn and winter specials are always a hit and between mini-Easter eggs in a nest and crumbles in a pumpkin, we can't wait to see what it comes up with next.

Mercato Metropolitano
and Mercato Mayfair

CENTRAL AND WEST LONDON FOOD HALLS WITH ITALIAN HEART

⊖ Elephant & Castle/Marble Arch

The brainchilds of the Mercato Metropolitano team, who started in Milan in 2015, London's south-based Mercato Metropolitano and central Mercato Mayfair are two of the city's most popular food halls. The former, the original location, is situated on an abandoned paper factory site in Elephant and Castle and is popular with young Londoners, especially on weekends and for after-work drinks; the latter is nestled in a stunning deconsecrated central London church and is more popular with tourists.

Mercato Metropolitano, London's first sustainable community market, is huge. The best feature, in our opinion, is the outdoor courtyard, full of lush leaves and fairy lights and perfect for dining out on a spring day. Foodwise you are really spoiled for choice. Try Dez Amore's fresh pasta, Fresco La Pizza's Neapolitan pizza, Badiani's ice cream, Little Sicily for cannoli and arancini, and Korean Green Choi's authentic pancakes, among other delights.

Mercato Mayfair, on the other hand, is a great escape from London's rainy weather. The Grade-I listed former St Mark's Church on North Audley Street now hosts a variety of cuisines across two floors, a vaulted crypt in the basement that hosts a wine cellar and a sushi bar and even a secret rooftop terrace. Our favourite part, though, are the two bars at the altar, where you can grab a G&T from, yes, Jim & Tonic, or an Aperol spritz from BeBeMe to drink with your pizza from Fresco (our favourite stall!).

Kingly Court

CARNABY'S BEST KEPT AL FRESCO SECRET

⊖ Oxford Circus

Kingly Court is Carnaby's best kept secret, a three storey-high dining experience. It's hard to believe that this colourful courtyard has managed to remain so hidden, as it's in such a touristy area, but head here any day of the week and you will mainly find Londoners enjoying food and drinks from one of the many international restaurants, cafés or bars.

During summer, Kingly Court is a buzzy al fresco hangout, while in winter the space is covered and offers an escape from Carnaby's bustle. You really are spoilt for choice as to where to dine, so we are going to help you out with a few of our favourites. For lunch, we absolutely love Imad's Syrian Kitchen, run by Imad Alarnab who is a Syrian chef, entrepreneur and refugee who ran successful restaurants, juice bars and cafés in Damascus, all destroyed by the war. The sharing plates and cocktails are very tasty, while there is a general fun and vibrant vibe on this top floor restaurant.

Le Bab, on the second floor, overlooking the terrace, is also a great option if you want a 'fancy' kebab, combining the flavours of the Middle East, East and Far East. For dinner, we love Señor Ceviche, a Nikkei Peruvian restaurant and Pisco bar, on the first floor. And talking about bars, Nightjar is a must if you like live music – from jazz and blues to funk and swing, while Cahoots is set in a Blitz bunker in a pretend Tube station (yes, you read correctly!) where you can enjoy cocktails out of hip flasks, milk bottles and tins and eat 1940s rationed snacks. Wooden escalators lead you down to a stationmaster at an entry kiosk.

Also, don't be surprised if you see many people eating a Pizza Pilgrims' Neapolitan pizza on one of the many outdoor tables on the warmer days. You will probably want to join them!

AFTERNOON

Arcade Hall, Battersea

FROM POWER STATION TO FOODIE DESTINATION

 Battersea Power Station

The redevelopment of Battersea Power Station has been one of the most impressive restoration projects of the past decade in London. What used to pump out fumes, just fifty years ago, has now become a favourite foodie destination. Managing to maintain the charm of the Grade II-listed building on the outside, the Arcade Hall provides a plethora of international flavours inside.

This huge canteen-style space takes you back to the 1970s, with vintage vinyl hanging on the walls, neon and retro music playing on the speakers. The cuisine is international, with thirteen different vendors. You can order anything from pizza, stir-fries and salads, Cantonese comfort food, bao, sushi, gelato to Nepalese street food. Anything. One of our favourite features is that everything can be ordered via a QR code, which means you can do a pick and mix of different cuisines without having to queue at the stalls. Assuming the WiFi works.

Battersea Brewery, the first micro-brewery by the team behind Mosaic Pubs, is also based here, with a taproom on site; it also serves a host of craft beers from international and south London breweries, plus a selection of wines. The ABC Bar serves classic cocktails from around the world.

Generally, Arcade Hall has a great, fun vibe, making it the perfect place for catching up with friends, and every Thursday, Friday and Saturday it hosts resident DJs from eight 'til late, with funk, soul, disco and R&B tracks.

Victoria Market Hall

FORMER DANCE HALL TURNED FOODIE DESTINATION

Victoria

Right opposite Victoria Station is a beautiful Edwardian building that almost seems abandoned. You would easily walk by and wonder what used to go on inside, back in the day, and you may even Google it to find out.

You will be pleasantly surprised to discover that it used to be a dance hall, but now is an incredible three-floor food hall. Inside are eleven kitchens, a coffee shop and three bars, and the best part of all is the rooftop terrace. Street food includes egg sandwiches by Eggslut (see page 12), Whipped London's artisan New York-style baked cheesecakes and frozen soft serve cheesecake, and DF Tacos for your taco fix.

To add to the vibe, the venue goes back to being a dance hall at the weekend, complete with live music and a line-up of DJs, vocalists and musicians.

AFTERNOON

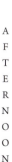

Bloomberg Arcade

A ROMAN DINING
BOULEVARD IN THE
SQUARE MILE

Cannon Street

Bloomberg Arcade is a charming dining boulevard built along the path of an old Roman street in the heart of the Square Mile – some 14,000 Roman artefacts were rescued during its excavation, with a number now on show to the public. Set on the site of Bloomberg's European headquarters, it features a number of fantastic restaurants and bars, in addition to staging regular events from music to public art, supported by Bloomberg's art and cultural partners.

As for the eateries, our favourite breakfast spot is Caravan (see page 44). Vinoteca is a great spot for people-watching while sipping on a glass of red and enjoying a plate of gnocchi, or if you want to try (fancy) BBQ and street food from around India, head to Brigadiers, inspired by an Indian army mess hall, from the team behind Gymkhana. As for dinner, we always love to dine at vibrant Lina Stores, for small pasta-sharing plates in their pastel-coloured restaurant.

Mare Street Market

Hackney Central

Mare Street Market is one of east London's coolest hangouts. Right in the heart of London Fields and next-door neighbour to Netil 360 (see page 162), you will find everthing from a fancy record store, a florist, a tattoo parlour, a café, a miniature liquor store to even a little studio created to register podcasts.

The décor is of a classic warehouse, open plan, with tall ceilings and lots of natural light. During the day, there are many young professionals working on their laptops, complete with their dogs, drinking flat whites and Matcha lattes. In the evening, the scene changes completely, with people mingling while drinking Negronis and craft beers.

The showstopper is the over-the-top Dining Room, full of vintage objects, statues and Pure White Lines' chandeliers, which are all for sale. Here you can enjoy a salad or a Neapolitan pizza, which seems to be its speciality.

Also noteworthy is the fairy lights terrace, which is buzzing during the summer months!

Brick Lane

VIBRANT, DIVERSE FOOD IN AN AUTHENTIC LOCATION

⊖ Shoreditch High Street

This area in east London is one of the most multiculturally diverse and exciting in the whole of London. A draw for new immigrants to Britain, with its close proximity to the docks and cheap housing, Brick Lane is today a melting pot of the very different communities who have set up shop here – literally – since the sixteenth century.

The Huguenots fleeing France, the Irish fleeing famine and persecution, the Jews fleeing the Inquisition and various pogroms and the Nazis, Indians and Bangladeshis, to more recently Somalis and East Europeans, all settled here. And out of this rich cultural diversity a vibant food culture has emerged, celebrating the cuisines of the areas from which these people originated, and a fusion of these cultures, too. From unfussy curry joints and street food joints to the famous all-night bagel shops, prepare for your tastebuds to have quite the journey around the world.

To most people, though, nothing says Brick Lane more than curry houses, a distinctive mark of years and years of Bangladeshi migration here, so much so it's known as Banglatown. Lined up in the main road, the majority of these family-run restaurants have been here since the 1960s, and still serve traditional food. Sheba – here since 1974 – is one of our favourites, perfect for those days when you really want to add some spice in your life. The menu includes Bangladeshi and Indian family recipes, such as delicious tandoori lamb, samosas, king prawn Malabar, along with Britain's favourite dish, a creamy tikka masala.

Brick Lane would not be Brick Lane, though, without its Jewish population – immigration to this area was so big that at the end of the nineteenth century a quarter of Spitalfield's population was Jewish. And migrants brought with them interesting new foods. Comforting salt beef bagels became iconic to Brick Lane's foodie scene, with people flocking from all over town to try them, especially to the east London institution Beigel Bake, open twenty-four hours and serving freshly baked bagels since 1974. And then there's its rival Beigel Shop, established in 1855. Everyone has a story of pitching up to refuel with a bagel after clubbing or a party, or early morning on a Sunday. Drawing celebrities, tourists, taxi drivers and locals alike, these are the places to come, but know what you want to order!

Between vintage stores, graffiti art and street markets, Brick Lane is one of the most exciting areas in town, we think, especially on a Sunday, when it draws visitors from nearby Columbia Road and Spitalsfield markets, too. Pay a visit to the Truman Brewery, once a derelict building, to find a unique mix of stores, markets and bars. Don't miss out on Upmarket for – you guessed it – more food and around forty stalls showcasing international food, indulgent desserts and independent little vendors, from Ethiopian and Korean to specialist bakery. Take your time to explore this unique area. Listen to great music, take in the smells, sounds, tastes and texture of a colourful area that continues to evolve and thrive.

BEIGEL BAKE

(1)

(2) BEIGEL SHOP

⊖ Shoreditch
High Street

THE TRUMAN
BREWERY

(3)

SHEBA RESTAURANT

(4)

UPMARKET BRICK
LANE FOOD HALL

(5)

BRICK LANE E.I.
ব্রিক লেন

⊖ Aldgate
East

AFTERNOON

PUBS

The Old Bank of England

BANKING ON A CLASSIC MEAL

⊖ Temple

We entered the Old Bank of England pub on Fleet Street almost by chance on a sunny spring day, intrigued by this impressive building that looked like it could have something interesting inside. And we surely weren't disappointed.

This pub resides in the old Law Courts' branch of the previous Bank of England, which operated between 1888 and 1975. The vaults once contained gold bullion and even the Crown Jewels, but even more interestingly, it was in the tunnels beneath the Old Bank of England that Sweeney Todd, demon barber of Fleet Street, supposedly butchered his victims before they were cooked and sold in pies to Mrs Lovett! That is why, among everything else, there is a small room that features two old barber chairs and lots of pictures featuring this story.

If the three large chandeliers, plastered ceilings and numerous artefacts spread around the pub aren't enough to convince you to go in, then maybe the vintage Routemaster double-decker bus in the summer garden may just do the trick. Ah, and the food is delicious too, far better than many pubs in the area, featuring old classics like ham, eggs and chips, a variety of pies and burgers, and British winter warmer puddings, like treacle tart and jam sponge, all made with great ingredients. There's also a non-gluten and children's menu, as well as a buffet.

No. Fifty Cheyne

FANCY SUNDAY CHELSEA ROASTS

⬤ Sloane Square

Located in Chelsea, right on the riverside, you'll notice No. Fifty Cheyne's bright and flower-adorned façade right away. The baby blue front complements the nearby pastel-hued Albert Bridge, making for the perfect photo opportunity. But this former pub is not all style and no substance: the food inside is seriously top-notch too.

The talented executive chef has created a menu based on hearty British dishes, with meat and fish cooked over the open-plan grill his specialty. Although a local, popular with Chelsea's distinguished residents, inside the vibe is anything but stuffy and the plush seating, candles and friendly staff will make you feel at home. Now, why are we recommending it? No. Fifty Cheyne's award-winning weekend roasts are why we are sending you here. They are the talk of neighbourhood and rightly so! Available both on Saturdays and Sundays, the roasts feature either a forty-day aged beef sirloin, a Cumbrian chicken or a roasted cauliflower steak as a veggie option. All come with myriad trimmings – glazed carrots, cabbage, roast potatoes and Yorkshire pudding. Of course. Oh, and loads and loads of gravy.

The full grill menu is also available if you prefer something more seasonal. Maybe start with some Isle of Wight asparagus with Cornish crab mayonnaise or Isle of Sky scallops, or create your own roast with any main from the grill (Dover sole, Châteaubriand or Surf & Turf with beef fillet and red prawns). The trimmings are an additional price.

No. Fifty Cheyne offers Saturday and Sunday roasts to take home. Just order the day before and enjoy your delicious fare in the comfort of your own home, on your own or with family and friends.

A
F
T
E
R
N
O
O
N

The Holly Bush

THE PRETTIEST PUB
IN HAMPSTEAD

⊖ Hampstead

Without a doubt, the Holly Bush, in lovely Hampstead, is one of the most charming pubs in the whole of London. With a quirky façade adorned with hanging baskets of flowers and century-old interiors, this historic pub will make you fall in love hard and fast.

Before becoming a pub in 1928, it was a residential house. Now, this Grade II-listed pub is enticing, full of cosy corners, the wooden oak rooms and the dark brown stools at the bar counter making it look like it's stuck in time. The best part is the working fireplace, where you can warm up after an afternoon spent walking about Hampstead on a crisp autumn or winter day. The food is good. The pub has an AA Rosette for culinary excellence. The menu blends classic pub dishes with extraordinary, seasonal and sustainable ingredients, such as classic roasts, Exmoor caviar, cucumber flowers with Chardannoy jelly, crispy pig's cheek, BBQ octopus and a vegetarian pithivier. Sounds good? Then head to the Holly Bush, grab a drink and get toasty by the fire.

This pub is also beautiful in the spring and summer time, so grab a seat outside in the bench area or join the people standing outdoors with a glass of wine to soak up the sun.

+ INSIDER TIP
〰〰〰〰

For the picture-perfect photo, head to the end of the cul-de-sac and you will immediately see the angle overlooking the pub.

The Cadogan Arms

A MUCH-LOVED CHELSEA INSTITUTION

⊖ Sloane Square

Having served the local Chelsea community for more than two centuries, the Cadogan Arms is – in our eyes – the perfect combination of comfort and class. Located on the iconic King's Road, it's a place where you can go all dressed up or just pop by for a roast in your jeans and sneakers.

Restored to its former glory after the original pub closed down, it now happily attracts returning locals, tourists and curious passers-by. The space inside is just beautiful, with a roaring fire in winter, comfy armchairs and jaw-dropping chandeliers. In true Chelsea style, the drinks and food menus are a combination of pub classics with a few fancy twists.

Its inventive cocktail menu showcases plenty of interesting takes on the classics, such as the Sticky Toffee Old Fashioned, made with Brown Butter Buffalo Trace, PX sherry and bitters sherbet or the Clementini, made with gin, Cointreau, clementine sherbet and lemon. There are also seasonal cocktails, such as a creamy Irish Coffee and a Mulled New York Sour. Don't miss out on the fun 'tiny chasers', 50 ml of frozen mini drinks designed to be enjoyed alongside a pint of beer.

In terms of food at the Cadogen, the menu ranges from starters and sharing dishes, such as black pudding Scotch eggs, Irish soda bread with Guinness butter and Jersey rock oysters, to abundant main course classics, such as beer battered fish and chips, beef and Guinness pie with clotted cream mashed potatoes and cider Fowey mussels. Sides include the almost compulsory skinny fries and grilled hispi cabbage. In addition, there are feasting menus for up to fifty to sixty people, vegetarian and omnivore.

On Sundays, it's roast time, of course. You can either get your own or order the meat selection board to share. Finish your meal with the signature fruit trifle showstopper.

AFTERNOON

The Churchill Arms

CHRISTMAS EXTRAVAGANZA

⊖ High Street Kensington/Notting Hill Gate

Chances are, if you have walked past the street that connects Notting Hill to Kensington, you have come across the Churchill Arms, instantly recognisable for its floral display. Built in 1750, the pub is one of the most historic in London. Legend says that in the 1800s Winston Churchill's grandparents were regulars here. Inside the pub is a cluster of Churchill and war memorabilia.

Now, the food is possibly not what you would expect from a pub of this kind. The first London pub to serve Thai food, it continues that tradition. The skilled chefs whip up tantalising regional delicacies such as the Pad Kee-Mao, made with stir-fried noodles, freshly chopped chilli, garlic and peppers, or the spicy red Panang curry, made of dried red chilli with coconut milk, Thai lime leaves and peppers.

No less than forty-two hanging flower baskets, one hundred tubs and forty-eight boxes on the windows adorn the façade of this pub, creating a riot of blooms and colours. During the festive period, though, is when the magic really happens. The flowers get replaced by almost one hundred Christmas trees and 11,500 lights, all switched on at night to maximise the impact of this Christmas extravaganza. We'll let you guess the energy bills!

The Duke of Cambridge

BRITAIN'S FIRST ORGANIC PUB

⊖ Angel

The Duke of Cambridge is located in leafy Islington, just a stroll away from the Regent's Canal and Angel's bustling Upper Street. With its rich blue façade and rustic wooden benches, this is the definition of a successful local gastropub.

Much loved by Islington residents, we adore this place so much we almost want to keep it a secret. Almost. Since 1998, the Duke of Cambridge has proudly been certified by the Soil Association to be Britain's first organic pub. This means that fresh and seasonal products are used with sustainable methods of cooking and sourcing, and transparency with its suppliers. Now on to the fun stuff! If you are thirsty, you can enjoy a great selection of craft beers, organic wines and vibrant cocktails. The food menu is constantly changing to keep up with seasonality and availability.

In summer, expect refreshing items like aubergine zaalouk, with quinoa, courgette and cauliflower tahini, or cauliflower with black garlic dressing and hazelnuts. Only the finest cuts of meat and day boat fish are paired with seasonal vegetables. For dessert, we can't think of anything better than the Basque cheesecake with orange curd, slowly savoured while basking in the sun.

AFTERNOON

The George

THE BEST IRISH COFFEE IN LONDON

Great Portland Street/
Oxford Circus

The George is a gorgeous eighteenth-century and Grade II-listed pub which has been recently refurbished to perfection. Located on Great Portland Street in Fitzrovia, it makes for the perfect place for after-work drinks. Followed by dinner, of course.

From the Green Room and the Snug on the ground floor to the upstairs Private Dining Room, all the dining rooms are irresistible. Start your meal with snacks such as Welsh rarebit croquettes and cured salmon tartare with Irish soda bread. Mains range from a paneer curry to a very British ploughman's, traditionally made with Cheddar, pickles and vegetables, ham hock and a crispy baguette. Indulgent sandwiches include a fried chicken sandwich, as well as a vegetarian option with chilli, coriander and melting cheese. On Sundays, there is also the option of a scrumptious roast made up of all the usual classics.

The menu is completed by a tiny yet mighty selection of puddings, such as the loveliest of sticky toffee puddings – accompanied by Cornish clotted cream. The star of the show, however, is the Irish coffee. The recipe is top secret, but we do know that its deliciousness has something to do with the Guinness reduction they use. Enjoy it upstairs for a true moment of peace. But just don't expect to go back to the office.

The Italian Greyhound

ITALIAN BACARI
AND POOCHES

Marble Arch

The Italian Greyhound is a cosy neighbourhood restaurant in Marylebone. As the name indicates, it serves Italian food and is super dog-friendly. To the extent that we have heard that they often organise doggie reunions for the neighbourhood's pooches.

It can easily be confused for a chic pub from the outside, with its whitewashed Victoria exterior and beautiful striped canopies, but as soon as you open the menu you realise that it's not fish and chips for you today. In fact, you will see a wide selection of Italian bacari, small dishes you would usually only see on the busy streets of Venice. An extensive Italian wine list complements the food, and the romantic atmosphere calls for the perfect date night.

During summer it is a pleasure to sit outside and sip a glass of wine or Aperol spritz, watching life go by. With your doggie, of course.

The Spaniards Inn

THE MOST HAUNTED PUB IN LONDON

⊖ Hampstead

Built in 1585, by two brothers from Spain, this now Grade II-listed, popular pub inspired no less than novelist Charles Dickens and poet John Keats. Interestingly, highwayman Dick Turpin was born here during the early 1700s, when his father was the landlord of the inn. Or so they say.

The interiors have been lovingly preserved, with loads of wood panelling and an open fire which creates a nostalgic and romantic atmosphere. In summer, the walled garden is a dream for al fresco dining or to enjoy a glass of wine in the sunshine. Its location in Hampstead makes it the perfect place to start (or end) a walk discovering the village. Lovely Kenwood House is nearby and so are the swimming ponds of Hampstead Heath.

The fare is classic pub grub, such as a Scotch egg with piccalilli, to finer fare such as shredded duck salad with mooli, and ribeye steak. Vegetarians and plant-based diets are also catered for.

Did we say that the pub comes up on every list of London's most haunted pubs? Keep an eye out for our friend Dick Turpin, a murdered Spanish dueller named Juan and the woman in white.

The Surprise

CHELSEA'S FAVOURITE GASTROPUB

⊖ Sloane Square

Around since 1853, the Surprise is a perfect little gastropub, hidden on a side street of Chelsea. When we stumbled across this pub on a walk during the Chelsea Flower Show, we thought, 'Oh, what a surprise, indeed!' Secluded from all the chaos of nearby King's Road, it is the perfect place to retreat and enjoy a glass of wine.

Preparing seasonal and local produce, along with an adventurous wine list and refreshing cocktails, the Surprise is very much a landmark in the area. It's had a major spruce up thanks to the new ownership of Jack, heir to the Greenall brewing dynasty.

With warm terracotta walls, loads of wooden touches (a nod to its naval past) and olive green leather booths, talented interior designer Isabella Worsley has done a marvellous job in combing elegance with warmth. The Hamilton Room is available to book for parties and drinks receptions – Chelsea residents love to celebrate their birthdays here! As for food, the Surprise prides itself on using the best of ingredients. The head chef loves to change the menu regularly and present new specials daily. From steaks to interesting vegetarian creations, such as baked harissa aubergine and locally sourced fish, you'll be fed and watered well and treated warmly and kindly.

A
F
T
E
R
N
O
O
N

Ye Olde Cheshire Cheese

A DICKENSIAN TIME-WARP MACHINE

Farringdon/St Paul's

One of London's oldest and most historic pubs, Ye Olde Cheshire Cheese has stood its ground in Fleet Street for centuries. Originally a chophouse, this was a place where customers would pop by to purchase a chop of meat and drink a pint of beer.

Like many other establishments, it was burnt down in 1666, during the Great Fire of London, but it was quickly rebuilt the following year. With a Dickensian vibe and moody, dark interiors, this pub is probably what first comes to mind when people think of a classic London pub. Interestingly, there is almost no natural light inside and no phone reception, making it a truly immersive experience. With its location in London's literary district, it attracted the likes of Charles Dickens and Sir Arthur Conan Doyle – Dickens even based part of *A Tale of Two Cities* in the Chop Room.

As for food, the pub pays a nod to its origins, serving hearty British food, like devilled kidneys and steak and kidney suet pudding. Vegetarian dishes include wild mushroom and spinach crumpet, cheese rarebit and a special Chop House Salad.

Today, patrons can choose to sit in a variety of rooms connected by labyrinth-like passageways and stairs, spread over four levels. Each of them has its own unique atmosphere. We love the open fireplace in winter, and the cellar, reachable only through a tiny alley. Typical, wonderful London.

The Cavendish

MARYLEBONE'S
ALL-YEAR ROUND
AL FRESCO GASTROPUB

⊖ Baker Street

The Cavendish, tucked away off Marylebone High Street, is an independent gastropub with seriously delicious food. Experimental cocktails, ever-changing seasonal dishes and one of the best Sunday roasts in the area are just a few of the characteristics that draw punters to this neighbourhood spot.

Its stylish al fresco-heated terrace is what caught our attention, though, in the first place. There is a more formal dining room and a lounge bar upstairs. The service is friendly but professional, so if you are up for a chat your waiter will definitely be up for one too. The menu is flavour-packed and dishes like seaweed dough balls, seabream carpaccio and twenty-eight-day aged ribeye are elegantly put together, as are the roasts, which include the usual suspects plus some surprises like roasted cornfed poussin and spinach and mushroom pithivier.

And in keeping with a neighbourhood local, dogs are not just welcomed here, they are treated like royalty and presented with a carefully curated dog-approved special menu, including appetisers, main courses and treats. In true Marylebone style!

A
F
T
E
R
N
O
O
N

The Audley Public House

FOR AFTER WORK DRINKS

⊖ Hyde Park Corner

The Audley Public House is set in a jaw-dropping listed Victorian building on the corner of Mayfair's South Audley Street. It has been recently restored by talented designers and architects to create a place where history and art go hand-in-hand. This is the place to go after work for a pint of beer or cider, while mingling with returning customers and suited-up office workers.

The first thing you'll see when you walk in is the stunning pink geometric ceiling by London-based artist Phyllida Barlow. It blends perfectly in with the nineteenth-century ceiling clock. Did you know it took eight weeks and a team of six polishers from France to restore it back to its glory?

Other interesting original features include the very carving knife (now framed on the wall) used when the pub first opened in 1888, an original fireplace and a shiny piano on the corner used for jazz nights. If you are famished, you can order the likes of Scotch eggs, oysters or coronation crab on toast. We've heard their Sunday roast is pretty great; do try it out for us and let us know how it is.

The Walmer Castle

NOTTING HILL LOCAL PUB

⊖ Notting Hill Gate

A Notting Hill landmark since 1845, this pub was named after the famous castle in Kent where the Duke of Wellington had recently died. The Walmer Castle has been serving generations of locals since then, welcoming this iconic neighbourhood's unique and diverse community for Sunday roasts and pints.

Recently refurbished, today it's one of the cosiest spots in Notting Hill. The pub features three floors of warm and stylish décor, with the highlights being the horseshoe-shaped bar, the fireplace and the wine wall on the first floor, inspired by antique apothecary cabinets. The menu is seasonal and modern British, with simple, tasty dishes created with the finest of local produce. The wine list is a whole different ball game, with an extensive wine list full of wines from small independent producers from all over the world. That must have taken ages to put together!

It's really well hidden, even though it's just by Portobello Road, which means it gets pretty busy with locals, which only adds to the atmosphere. Definitely one to keep in mind for your next stroll in this colourful neighbourhood.

Best Pizzas

London has come such a long way when it comes to pizza. Today the capital is packed with incredible pizzerias and we've had some of the best ones in our lives right here. Some places directly fly over Neapolitan pizzamakers from Italy and some have learned the art. Here is a selection of our favourite ones.

'O VER

'O ver, meaning 'truth' in Neapolitan dialect, serves authentic wood-fired Neapolitan pizza in a stylish setting. Their fare is very light and easy to digest, thanks to the unique use of seawater from the Mediterranean. Along with the classics, you can also find gourmet pizzas with the likes of the Ostuni with fior di latte mozzarella from Monti Lattari, yellow cherry tomatoes from Vesuvio, basil and topped with burrata, or the Primavera, again toped with Mortadella, Bronte's pistachio pesto and crushed pistachios. Locations in St James's and Borough.

RUDY'S PIZZA

Coming directly from Manchester, this much-loved pizza joint has taken Soho by the storm. With pillowy Neapolitan dough and high-quality toppings imported from Italy, baked in traditional Neapolitan ovens, this pizza is to be enjoyed sitting outside with a refreshing Aperol spritz in hand.

CINQUECENTO PIZZERIA

Founders Emanuele and Melo came from Italy with the dream of building an authentic Neapolitan pizzeria, and so they did in Chelsea, and also Portobello. The freshly prepared dough is left to rise for up to forty-eight hours. The Pizza della Nonna, made with DOP tomato sauce, smoked mozzarella, aubergines and Nonna's meatballs, is a firm favourite of ours. We also recommend the excellent appetisers.

DAROCO

Brought over to London from Paris, you are in safe hands with Daroco's Italian pizzamaker and Instagram-worthy blue butterfly oven. Daroco's pizzas are incredible, coming straight from the Neapolitan school, with fluffy crusts and generous toppings. You can choose from classics such as Parmigiana pizza to curious ones like the Iodizalizioso Verde, made with asparagus cream, fior di latte, wild garlic leaves, burrata and bottarga.

50 KALÒ DI CIRO SALVO

Voted best pizza in Europe numerous times, this award-winning restaurant has set up shop in Trafalgar Square. Renowned master pizzamaker Ciro Salvo makes sure his pizzas are topped with the very best ingredients and the dough is slowly fermented. We love the Nerano, made with provolone, creamed and diced courgettes, fior di latte and Colline Salernitane extra virgin olive oil, or the Gialla provola e pepe, with casa Marrazzo yellow 'Piennolo' tomatoes, provola smoked cheese and black pepper.

L'ANTICA PIZZERIA DA MICHELE

The offshoot of the Eat, Pray, Love pizzeria in Naples, it is famous for its huge pizzas. Nominated for best pizza in the world, the pizzerias are currently located in Soho and Baker Street in the UK. Stick to the classic Margherita to feel just like Julia Roberts.

SANTA MARIA

Founders Angelo and Pasquale opened up Santa Maria, originally in Ealing, west London, after working in pizzerias all over London, making Neopolitan pizzas the same way you'd find them in any street in their city. As well as excellent classics, there is whole vegan menu, with their housemade vegan mozzarella being the star of the show.

AFTERNOON TEA

The Zetter Clerkenwell

AFTERNOON TEA IN THE MAD HATTER'S LIVING ROOM

⊖ Farringdon

If you are looking for a quirky afternoon tea, then look no further. The Zetter Clerkenwell is a beautiful boutique hotel nestled inside a Georgian townhouse in one of London's oldest squares, St John's Square. Think of sipping tea surrounded by antique furniture, almost as if you were sitting in the Mad Hatter's living room.

The home takes its name from Wilhelmina Zetter, who was born in the 1700s (that is how old this townhouse is) and spent her life travelling around the world, yet called Clerkenwell home her whole life.

You enter through a large blue door and it has the feel of a secret spot that only a local would know about. The menu is interesting, making the most of seasonal and UK ingredients, with delicate sandwiches featuring Somerset brie, apricot and beetroot, and coronation smoked Norfolk chicken. There is a haggis and Kilverrock sausage roll and a whipped Kinderton ash goat's cheese quiche. Sweets include raisin and cinnamon buttermilk scones – as well as the regular kind – and Mojito macarons. The cocktails are as creative as the interiors, and we tried the Breakfast at Tiffany's, featuring croissant liquor, Jaques Picard and champagne, and the Piña Colada Royale, which mixes coconut and pineapple infused rum with champagne.

Definitely a must if you are looking for something unusual and different.

Fortnum & Mason

THE UNDISPUTED HOME OF LONDON'S AFTERNOON TEA

⊖ Green Park/Piccadilly Circus

For over a century, the majestic building of Fortnum & Mason has been the destination for afternoon tea. Hosted in the iconic Diamond Jubilee Tea Salon, this afternoon tea is the epitome of sophistication and old-school splendour. Previously, the Tea Salon was the Fortnum family's apartment and antique store. Today it provides the elegant location for a relaxed and timeless afternoon tea, much loved by visitors. Tea is taken very seriously here so it shouldn't come as a surprise that there is an in-house Tearista available for a tableside tea tasting experience. An organic sparkling tea has also been created that looks just like champagne but with zero alcohol, and mocktails are infused with their most popular blends.

Savoury lovers will be pleased to know that there is a full savoury afternoon tea, with a selection of savoury patisserie, on offer. All scones come with their signature strawberry preserve and lemon curd, while the sandwiches have classic flavours such as coronation chicken, Cotswold egg and mayonnaise, Suffolk-cured ham and cucumber with minted pea cream cheese.

The patisserie is ever-changing and crafted according to season. Tip: if you find yourself in the City, craving an afternoon tea, you can head inside the Royal Exchange and find yourself a mini version of Fortnum's afternoon tea.

Located inside the Marriott Hotel County Hall, The Library Lounge boasts enviable views over the Elizabeth Tower, the Houses of Parliament and River Thames. Talk about an afternoon tea with a view and, of course, it's landmark themed.

Centrally located on the South Bank, right next to the London Eye, this is the perfect spot for any tourist looking for an elegant break in a tiring day of sightseeing. There is so much to see in London after all! The building is historic in itself. Opened in 1922 by King George V, County Hall was originally used as a seat of government. After tasteful refurbishment, it has been restored and reopened as a hotel, keeping many original features, including the beautiful wooden floor and panelling.

The traditional oak bookcases, filled with literary rarities, stand proud in the room, bringing the space to life and reminding us of the original purpose of the room. Formerly, this was the private library of London's County Council members. Lucky them!

Afternoon tea comes with signature cakes, such as a miniature Elizabeth Tower brownie made with banana and chocolate, the round clock and of course the iconic Big Ben bell. The buttery brioche bun filled with Burford Brown truffled egg mayo got us asking for seconds and the sweet basil scones with tangy lemon curd countered the more classic golden raisin ones.

Enjoying one of the most quintessentially British traditions, overlooking the city's leading iconic landmarks, truly immersed us in the past. It's an experience that should be high up on everyone's London bucket list!

The Library at County Hall

A LANDMARK VIEW

⊖ Waterloo

One Aldwych

CHARLIE AND THE CHOCOLATE FACTORY-THEMED AFTERNOON TEA

🚇 Charing Cross/Covent Garden

This afternoon tea is really one for that inner child! The Charlie and the Chocolate Factory afternoon tea at One Aldwych is every chocolate lover's dream. Located right in the heart of London, this former turn of the century newspaper-building-turned-luxury-hotel provides an afternoon tea that transforms the ordinary into extraordinary, making you feel like you are right in the middle of Willy Wonka's world. So, step into a magical space of bubbles and adventure!

This is an adventurous but tasty experience, from fizzy drinks (or champagne) and caramel teas to mini chocolate milkshakes – mixed by a waterfall, of course – and a savoury not-quite-as-it-seems beetroot macaron, a snoozzberry jam to go with your scones and 'hair toffee' mousse. All stacked up in a wooden box comes the fluffy floss – strictly not for dentists – and an array of scrumptious sweets.

This place is very much child-friendly, perfect for a day out with your family or for a date with your sweet other half. After indulging in one of the tastiest tales ever told, it's easy to leave feeling just like a blown-up Violet Beauregarde!

The Cadogan

TEATIME,
À LA FRANÇAISE

⊖ Sloane Square

It's in the incredibly beautiful setting of the Cadogan in Sloane Street that you will enjoy a remarkable and imaginative French take of the classic traditional English afternoon tea. Enter the Cadogan Lounge, where a tranquil and elegant atmosphere awaits you. Relax and unwind while letting the knowledgeable staff talk you through the menu, where passion and creativity unite. Brainchild of renowned pastry chef and *Bake-Off* judge Benoît Blin, this afternoon tea is distinctively seasonal and has a French twist. Benoît's knowledge comes from working alongside chef-patron Raymond Blanc at the Cadogan's sister Belmond hotel and two Michelin-starred Manoir Aux Quat'Saisons.

The menu weaves in the chef's culinary stories and family memories, using only the best seasonal ingredients available in the UK. The traditional sandwiches are replaced by a selection of open ones, including a salmon gravadlax on toasted croissant with quail egg and a Cornish crab brioche with pink grapefruit.

For the sweet course, we recommend the ultra lemon cake. It's what each guest finds in the room at the sister hotel in the countryside – a tradition for over thirty years. And, of course, no afternoon tea would be complete without the tea itself. There's an excellent selection of black and green teas and tissanes, as well as champagnes. A very fine experience indeed.

AFTERNOON

Brigit's Bakery

AFTERNOON TEA BUS TOURS WITH A TWIST

⊖ Leicester Square/Victoria

We can't think of anything more quintessentially British than a red double-decker bus and afternoon tea. Can you? Brigit's Bakery, based in Covent Garden, has answered all our prayers with its Afternoon Tea Bus Sightseeing Tours. While riding on one of the vintage Routemaster buses, we can sip tea or drink a cheeky G&T while sightseeing London.

Departing from either Victoria Coach Station, Trafalgar Square or Victoria Embankment, each tour lasts around 90 minutes, giving you all the time you need to enjoy mouthwatering cakes, tasty sandwiches and scones, while spotting the city's top sights and choosing those Insta-worthy moments.

Apart from the regular tours, Brigit's Bakery-run themed events including the cutest Peppa Pig and Paddington Bear afternoon teas for children. You can also hire out the entire bus for your own private tea party, so perfect for birthdays, hen dos or graduations! It's a fun experience and the skilled team on the bus makes it extra special. When booking, we recommend you pick a seat on the top deck of the bus for the best views of the city!

Covent Garden Hotel

A PEOPLE-WATCHING AL FRESCO AFTERNOON TEA

⊖ Covent Garden

The Covent Garden Hotel is a quaint hotel located in the heart of theatreland, a stone's throw away from the bustling piazza that shares its name. It is one of our favourite places to stop for coffee – and it is just as perfect for afternoon tea.

Tea is served in the polished Brasserie Max, an elegant room designed by resident decorator Kit Kemp and filled with cosy nooks, dark wooden touches and medieval-style chandeliers. Although lovely, if the weather is nice, we recommend grabbing a seat outside to enjoy an al fresco experience at one of the best people-watching locations in town. Facing bustling Monmouth Street, the terrace is ideal for you to savour your afternoon tea in total peace while watching the world go by.

Served in beautifully adorned china, it includes a selection of well-researched teas, including the expected, Breakfast and Earl Grey, to the intriguing, such as Tall Trees, with its citrus and herby notes – we are particularly partial to the rooibos, orange and cactus fig one. From the selection of sandwiches and pastries, you can expect traditional but delicious flavours, with the chamomile and blueberry Opera cake and the Victoria sponge among our favourites.

Given its location, this afternoon tea works really well as a pre-dinner treat, too.

The Landmark London

UNDER THE PALM TREES

⊖ Baker Street

Located in Marylebone, the Landmark London is a historic hotel originally opened in 1899 as the Grand Central Hotel. It was the last of the great Victorian railway hotels, built with the purpose of serving the nearby Marylebone Station's passengers. Nowadays, this stunning hotel combines timeless British elegance with contemporary flair, welcoming guests from all over the world.

The hotel's pièce de résistance is the impressive glass-roofed atrium, adorned with towering palm trees which will make you wonder if you are still in London. It's right here in the Victoria Winter Garden that afternoon tea is served. The menu has been choreographed by pastry chefs Mauro Di Lieto and Daniel Schevenels, the winners of *Bake Off: The Professionals* 2023 to create a mouth-watering experience. It has received an Award of Excellence, so you know already that this will be delicious.

With a menu that changes seasonally, get ready to indulge in a tempting selection of sensory delights, including a Valrhona dark chocolate tart with rosemary and apricot jam or a choux bun with salted pistachio cream and sour cherries, and then there are the lemon and blueberry scones to die for. The organic egg mayo with black truffle and chives sandwich is one to reorder once, maybe twice, with absolutely no shame at all. The atmosphere is relaxed, but the high palms and the mellow sound of the piano filtering through makes this tea quite a magical experience.

Brown's Hotel

TEA IN LONDON'S FIRST HOTEL

⊖ Green Park

Located in beautiful Mayfair, just off London's Green Park, is Brown's Hotel. This fascinating, historic establishment dates back to the 1832. It is right here in the Drawing Room that Queen Victoria is believed to have enjoyed her ritual afternoon tea. We really cannot blame her, as the afternoon tea at Brown's is one of the best in the capital.

Here, old-school glamour meets contemporary London, resulting in a welcoming yet elegant tea experience. Even the décor is a medley of the two. Original wood panelling and exposed fireplaces juxtapose the trendy Paul Smith lighting and fashionable fabrics. To feel just like royalty, relax with the music from the grand piano, with a glass of champagne in one hand and soft scones filled with cream and jam in the other.

The finger sandwiches – replenished until you get full – are made with traditional flavours such as coronation chicken, pickled cucumber and devilled egg mayonnaise, yet there is also a full plant-based menu available. The pastries are a dream, and just when you think you can't eat any more, get ready for the signature cakes, varying from Victoria sponge to Kipling cake. All in all, Brown's manages to put on a quintessentially English afternoon tea experience while still seeming modern and up to speed with the outside world.

AFTERNOON

The Dorchester

A VERY FESTIVE AFTERNOON TEA

⊖ Green Park

Afternoon tea at the Dorchester is something not to be missed, but Christmas afternoon tea, well . . . Set in the Promenade, the restaurant that runs the length of the hotel; this is an experience that will get you right in the festive spirit.

A London institution since 1931, the Dorchester really had time to master the art of this fine English afternoon ritual. During December, the whole hotel gets decorated with joyful Christmas trees and themed installations, bringing smiles to hotel residents and visitors alike. The opulent Promenade creates the most inviting space to savour the joys of an elegant but relaxing afternoon tea, created by award-winning pastry chef Michael Kwan, and accompanied by the tones of the in-house pianist.

The Christmas version of a daily classic features the likes of mulled pear, spiced beetroot and brie tart, and delicate sandwiches with English cucumber and pine cream or turkey, cranberry, chestnut and pork stuffing on malt bread. Warm scones arrive next, followed by a seasonal treat created by the talented chefs here. The final course is also the most awaited: a selection of themed pastries so sweet they will make your heart melt. They change every year but at the time we visited we were presented with the likes of a delicious Mont Blanc with chestnut cream and an almost too-pretty-to-eat shiny Santa hat. Make the afternoon tea at the Dorchester your new festive tradition, one to cherish with your family and loved ones. Glass of chilled champagne in hand, of course.

The Lane

A TRULY THEATRICAL AFTERNOON

⊖ Leicester Square

Set inside the iconic Theatre Royal Drury Lane – the oldest used theatre site in the world – this elegant afternoon tea will take you straight back to the splendour of the Regency era. Tea is served in the Grand Saloon on the upper floor of the theatre, under dazzling chandeliers and among marble columns.

Dine on fine bone china plates and teacups, representing different mythical characters and customised by British interiors designers Kit and Willow Kemp. The menu is decadent, created by expert artisan baker Lily Vanilli, 'Queen of Cakes'. The tea is very much sweet-orientated, with cute little pastries and miniature sticky puddings taking centre stage. In the savoury section, don't expect traditional sandwiches. You'll find three bites created by their in-house chefs, such as a mind-bending savoury take on the French classic madeleine, made with whipped feta and pickled heritage carrot, that has to be eaten to be believed. The triangular signature scones come to the table, warm and sprinkled with brown sugar, and the addition of whipped salted butter along the classic clotted creams and jams. The best part is the buttercream signature cake adorned with Lily's iconic icing and pastel colours, a real treat to get you in the right mood for your theatre show!

A
F
T
E
R
N
O
O
N

The Ritz

THE TEA OF ALL TEAS

Green Park/Piccadilly Circus

Ever wondered what is like to step inside the most iconic hotel in London? Afternoon tea at the Ritz is not only truly wonderful, it also gives you the perfect excuse for a good snoop around and feel like Julia Roberts for a day. With a long waiting list – it's the Ritz, after all – this is one to plan far in advance, so if you are visiting London we recommend securing a spot as soon as possible.

From the uniformed doormen complete with hats, white gloves and friendly smiles, to heavy revolving doors, this place screams luxury from the second you enter. The Palm Court, where tea is served, might put Versailles to shame with it's a gilded glory of mirrors, chandeliers and crisp white tablecloths. The staff are friendly and attentive but since the tea is so popular, they operate on seating slots to fit everyone in, with no delays. This means they are very organised, almost faultless, and yet this is not the place to linger and you can take your pastries home of course if you don't finish in time!

The plate of sandwiches – finely cut and delicate as you can imagine – is one of the most abundant we have ever seen, with the likes of cucumber with cream cheese, Scottish smoked salmon and egg mayonnaise in a brioche roll. Scones come warm with Cornish clotted cream and strawberry preserve, while the pastries are beautifully presented and can be replenished on request. If that's not enough for you, get ready for the Ritz tableside signature service, with two generous slices of mouth-watering seasonal cake served directly from a bespoke cake trolley.

The final ingredient that makes this unforgettable is the wonderful music from the resident pianist. In true Ritz style, don't forget to dress up for the occasion – suit and tie are requested for the gents and ladies are welcomed to don their favourite elegant attire. It's something we all need to do more often, and this is the perfect excuse to do so!

The Goring

A ROYAL WARRANTED AFTERNOON TEA

Victoria

The Goring, the last remaining family-owned luxury hotel in the whole of London, is also the closest hotel to Buckingham Palace. Since it opened its doors in 1910, it has been a favourite with the royal family. It's not surprising then, that it has been granted a royal warrant, a mark of recognition for businesses which supply goods and services to the royal households. It is the only hotel to retain such a recognition. Quite special, right?

The afternoon tea here is nothing less than fabulous, but then as the holder of the British Tea Guild Council's Top London Afternoon Tea Award and the Award of Excellence, it should be!

Featuring delectable seasonal pastries, warm scones with Devonshire clotted cream and a wide range of fine teas, the menu changes to provide the best seasonal ingredients. Tea is served daily on the sun-kissed the Veranda, overlooking the garden, which makes it a relaxing spot for a long overdue catch-up with friends while sipping from an array of teas (and champagne of course). Enjoy the plush yellow chairs; they are just adorable!

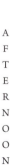

AFTERNOON

The Lanesborough

THEMED AFTERNOON TEA

⊖ Hyde Park Corner

Served in the majestic surroundings of the Lanesborough Grill, afternoon tea is truly an elegant affair. The baby blue, ornately decorated room is filled with natural light during the day thanks to the beautiful domed glass roof, while the opulent chandeliers are always softly lit to create a sense of warmth. We can't think of a better place to sip your tea and people watch!

Afternoon tea here is often themed around special occasions or current TV series, such as a Regency-inspired *Bridgerton*, or one paying homage to the movie *Cruella*. At Christmas, be ready for a winter extravaganza filled with seasonal treats. A favourite of ours is the Meadow, paying homage to spring and inspired by the flora and the fauna in the surrounding London parks. It really got us excited for the season ahead and to finally see the first signs of the season around us.

One thing that remains the same is the care and the attention to detail that the talented pastry team puts in this afternoon tea. The delicate pastries are so well-thought out and the team spends a long time coming up with ideas and flavours to fit each theme. Usually there is limited edition cocktail that comes with the tea, too, such as the Friends to Lovers Cocktail honouring Penelope Featherington, one of the protagonists in *Bridgerton*, or its non-alcoholic equivalent, the Blooming Wallflower. So, put on your best dress and get ready to feel like a member of the 'ton' for a day.

The Savoy

THE BEST PLACE TO EXPERIENCE LONDON AT CHRISTMAS TIME

⊖ Charing Cross/Embankment

A real treat at any time of the year, afternoon tea at this iconic hotel brings that extra magic during the festive season. The Savoy is the perfect base to explore London and see the city in all its festive glory. Nearby Covent Garden and the Strand are all wonderfully decorated at this time of year and the hotel definitely keeps up with its neighbours.

Afternoon tea takes place in the festively decorated Thames Foyer, which features a stunning glass dome and an intricate indoor gazebo, inside of, which the resident pianist enchants guests. The staff are so welcoming and attentive, and if you are celebrating something, they will treat you with extra special care.

The meticulously crafted menu includes an array of festive pastries and sandwiches designed to appraise the palate and the eyes. The flavours and shapes change every year according to the theme of the decorations, but they all feature classic and nostalgic flavours of the season. When you've finished, the Christmas lights will most probably be switched on, so go for a festive walk around Covent Garden or along the river to enjoy yuletime London.

A
F
T
E
R
N
O
O
N

Aqua Shard

A PETER PAN AFTERNOON IN NEVERLAND

⊖ London Bridge

With sweeping views across the City and a touch of fairytale nostalgia, the Aqua Shard on Level 31 of the Shard really puts on a spectacular display with its afternoon tea. Inspired by J.M. Barrie's popular fairy-tale, the Peter Pan Afternoon Tea encompasses all the magic through themed sweets and savouries, and its specially made teastand, inspired by the *Jolly Roger*, Captain Hook's pirate ship, which arrives in a floating cloud of dry ice for extra theatrical effect. Even teas and cocktails are in line with the story, with a specially curated Adventure Tea – a blend of mango, orange and ginger – and Fairy Dust and Never Grow Up as tipples.

Guests can choose from carefully curated and beautifully drawn map menus and all tastes are catered for, from the classic to vegetarian, vegan and pescatarian. The savouries are what come first. A chicken and crispy bacon sandwich is wrapped in paper denoting the 'Lost Boy Rules': no talking to pirates, believe in fairies, think happy thoughts and, of course, never grow up. For vegetarians, it's a Little Bird, an egg, watercress and truffle sarnie, and for the vegans, beetroot, vegan mayo and rocket. Easy, right? There is also an Enormous Mushroom Chimney, taking inspiration from the mushroom stools on Neverland island.

Warm scones are hidden in a treasure chest inside the vessel stand, as well as sweets and gummies of all sorts. Sweet apricot jam and coconut clotted cream make the scones really stand out. Tinker Bell is present too, taking her place high on the stand, in the form of an iced biscuit sprinkled with gold dust. The detail and storytelling of the famous novel will be much appreciated by all children – including those who have, regretfully, grown up.

The Stafford London

ST JAMES'S BEST KEPT SECRET

⊖ Green Park

The Stafford London, a truly charming hotel set just off Green Park, is the perfect little place to seek refuge from the world and enjoy a never-ending afternoon tea. It's one of only fifteen locations in London to be awarded the prestigious Award of Excellence in 2024, so you are in for a treat.

As soon as you step inside, the friendly staff will guide you to the Game Bird Lounge, a tranquil and informal room where tea is served. Here, you'll be greeted with a gorgeous silver champagne trolley and asked to make the first difficult choice between English sparkling wine, champagne brut or rosé. The tea menu is extensive, with all kinds of tea from all around the world. From the exquisite finger sandwiches to both sweet and savoury scones (made with Paxton & Whitfield Westcombe Cheddar), this afternoon tea is one to be enjoyed while taking all the time you need.

Seasonal pasties and cakes are theatrically served tableside and presented on a bespoke handcrafted wooden trolley. You are in the hotel where royals used to stay, after all. And if you are wondering why there is a pastry of a little white mouse, it's in honour of spy Nancy Wake, called the White Mouse for her ability to hide and sneak away from the Nazis during the Second World War. In the later part of her life, Nancy resided right here at the Stafford, where she would enjoy a daily gin and tonic in the American Bar.

A
F
T
E
R
N
O
O
N

Ice Creams

There is absolutely nothing better than an ice cream on a hot, sunny day in London! Granted, we don't get that many, but when we do, you need to have this covered. Move over the ubiquitious 99 Flake – here is our personal selection of the best ice creams in London town. And, yes, we're Italian so we know what we're talking about!

BADIANI 1932

This iconic Italian gelateria from Florence made everyone a little happier when it decided to open up in London. The creators of elevated signature flavour 'Buontalenti', made simply with cream, sugar and eggs, sell super creamy and seriously mouthwatering gelato. Our favourites are the Buontalenti pistachio and La Dolce Vita, with hazelnut and chocolate. Badiani's also sell seasonal delicacies such as Italian colomba and panettone. They have a range of vegan sorbets.

SPECIALITY CAFÈTIERE

This coffee shop in Hackney is where to go to satisfy your pistachio craze. It doesn't serve gelato as such, but it does have indulgent creations, such as the gelato-filled croissant and pistachio bombolone – an Italian doughnut filled with pistachio gelato and topped with pistachio sauce coming directly from a pistachio fountain. They can all be made to takeaway.

BILMONTE

Located in Soho, Bilmonte's gelato is the perfect drip temperature, the melting time never 'too fast' Try a little chocolate cone in one of the decadent flavours – gianduja, extra dark salted chocolate and double pistachio. It's worth it. This is also the home of the Bun-Brioscia, a Sicilian-style brioche filled with your choice of gelato and loads of whipped cream.

GELUPO

Offspring of acclaimed restaurant Bocca di Lupo, this Soho gelateria has become quite the hit. Expect lip-smacking gelato and sorbets with interesting flavours, including a rich and buttery salted caramel and pecan, a special Sicilian ricotta sour cherry and a chocolatey Rocher flavour. Sorbets include Alphonso mango, bitter chocolate or blood orange – all depending on the season, of course.

UNION ICE CREAM

Set in the pedestrianised Pavilion Road in Chelsea, this little parlour makes the finest ice creams and sorbets in the area. With a no-fuss approach and a big focus on ingredients, it hand-selects the best Sicilian blood oranges, makes its own honeycomb and sources milk from the Estate Dairy. Absolutely everything is made in-house and you can really tell. Flavours include cornflake, dulce de leche, honeycomb and Matcha. They even home deliver!

GELATERIA 3BIS

Served in London's oldest market, Borough Market, and in Portobello, Notting Hill – this is one for your late summer evenings. Open until late in summer, this gelateria, originating in Italy's Rimini Riviera, makes gelato in its on-sight laboratory. Favourite flavours include peanut butter, salted caramel and mascarpone and fig. Frozen yoghurt comes from the neighbouring Neal's Yard Dairy.

LA GELATIERA

La Gelateria in Covent Garden is home to experimental artisan gelato and sorbet, fusing ancient traditions with innovation. With flavours like strawberry prosecco granita, chocolate and chilli or honey, rosemary and orange zest, don't be afraid to try their playful combinations.

EVENING

DRINKS

Scarfes Bar

AN HOMAGE TO THE GREAT CARICATURIST

 Holborn

Tucked away in the Rosewood Hotel in London, Scarfes Bar is an elegant and stylish bar that is an absolute must for any Londoner or visitor. The bar is named after the renowned British caricaturist Gerald Scarfe, so it shouldn't surprise anyone that the walls are filled with his works, whether of the Beatles, Boris Johnson or a member of the royal family.

The ambience is cosy yet vibrant, with live jazz music playing from 8 p.m. every day of the week while people gossip over cocktails. Most guests dress for the occasion, so it's definitely not the kind of place where you can show up in your casual attire after a day out exploring London. Scarfes Bar doesn't accept reservations unless you are staying in the hotel, so if you don't like queuing it's probably advisable to go quite early, especially at the weekend.

+ INSIDER TIP

~~~~~~~~

If you are looking for a romantic date night or a cosy gossip session with friends, just head to Scarfes Bar and grab a leather chair by the roaring fire and settle in for the evening.

EVENING

La Fromagerie

A CHEESE LOVER'S PARADISE

Holborn/Russell Square

Set along vibrant Lamb's Conduit Street, one of London's best-kept secrets, La Fromagerie is a cheese enthusiast's paradise. Think boards with your favourite British, French or Italian cheese, raclette, fondue Savoyarde, gorgonzola, twice-baked soufflé and Camembert. All paired with wine, of course, sitting outside on a warm spring evening catching up with friends.

In addition to being a charming little restaurant, La Fromagerie is also a cheesemonger, where you can pick up and bring home over one hundred types of cheeses. Whether it's Colston Bassett Stilton you are looking for, Isle of Mull Cheddar, scamorza or Roquefort papillon, they really have it all.

La Fromagerie is part of a small family of cheeseries, the older siblings being based in Highbury and Marylebone. The shop in Marylebone, on Moxon Street, is also truly exceptional, with a maturing cellar, a dedicated walk-in cheese room and a cheese specialist to help with selections.

The on-site kitchen also produces homemade jams and chutneys, biscuits and cakes!

Booking Office 1869

A TRAIN STATION BAR
WITH GLAMOUR

King's Cross

Before heading to St Pancras International train station for one of our trips, we always end up scheduling a stop at the Booking Office 1869, set inside the St Pancras Renaissance Hotel London. This bar and restaurant are a reimagination of the station's original nineteenth-century ticket hall. The Victorian-style winter garden has a high-arching ceiling, large windows and tall palm trees, designed to give you that wow factor as soon as you step in.

The cocktail menu also takes inspiration from the Victorian-era, but here we prefer to drink a nice glass of champagne or English sparkling wine. It just gives us that vibe. There are DJ nights on Fridays and Saturdays, which makes for a fun night out after work, or spending the day at the Regent's Canal or shopping in the nearby charming Coal Drops Yard, just a short walk away.

EVENING

Mr Fogg's Society of Exploration

AN ADVENTUROUS DRINKING NIGHT OUT

Charing Cross

Mr Fogg's is a collection of extremely creative and fun bars around London. Each one has a theme, whether it's an old Victorian apothecary or a Cockney singalong tavern. Our absolute favourite, though, has to be Mr Fogg's Society of Exploration, where things really do get adventurous.

Think cocktails served in cappuccino cups and elephant tusks, a world-first automated Negroni-making machine, and bartenders dressed up in steampunk. The bar is located only a stone's throw away from Charing Cross station, where Phileas J. Fogg started his famous voyage around the world.

Inside you'll find wood-panelled walls, vintage leather seating and shelves filled with gadgets from his supposed travels. You can even have drinks in a life-size model of a Victorian steam train!

This speakeasy bar is the perfect spot for a fun night out with friends, maybe after dining in one of the many restaurants in Covent Garden. The drinks are very creative and imaginative – making for the perfect Insta-worthy moment – and the bar is open till late.

LSQ

AN OASIS IN ALL THE CHAOS

Leicester Square

If you have walked through the chaos that is Leicester Square and never noticed LSQ rooftop, we won't hold this against you, don't worry. Nestled in the Indigo Hotel, whether it's by day or by night, this space has one of the best views that London has to offer.

The atmosphere is fun and cheerful, with live music from emerging London artists. The cocktails, as you can imagine, reference some of London's iconic landmarks, many visible from the rooftop. Expect to see the Big Ben Fizz, the Mind the Gap, the Trafalgar Spritz and more.

The food menu is relaxed, with burgers, small bites and tasty desserts. The crowd can be quite mixed, with tourists who have stumbled upon it, Londoners taking visiting friends to impress them with the view and couples on a romantic date. It really is a place for everyone.

Ah, and lastly, as it's ideally placed in 'theatreland', it's a great spot for pre-theatre drinks and bites!

Florattica

FLOWER
ATTIC WITH
SPECTACULAR
VIEWS OF
THE CITY

Aldgate

Florattica is inspired by east London's rich textile industry, as you will notice as soon as you walk inside. The name plays with the words 'flower' and 'attic', so it's no surprise that the ceiling of this rooftop bar is adorned with silk woven floral patterns inspired by the seventeenth-century French Huguenots.

But as striking as the interiors may be, the real showstopper is the view, for us the best in the City of London. The skyline spans almost all of London's iconic skyscrapers, even St Paul's Cathedral is spectacularly visible in between the buildings.

As for the cocktails, they are of course all floral-inspired and very beautifully presented, and there's a wide-ranging wine and champagne menu, too. The food features sharing plates to enjoy while taking in the views and soaking up the alcohol. This hidden oasis on the eleventh floor really is the perfect place for spring and summer drinks, especially if the sun is shining.

The Coral Room

A COUNTRY HOUSE
TRANSPORTED
TO THE CITY

Russell Square

If you have walked along Great Russell Street and into the Coral Room at the Bloomsbury Hotel, you would never believe that this tranquil bar is just off Oxford Street's hustle and bustle. Designed by acclaimed Martin Brudnizki (who also designed Scarfes Bar, see page 149), this bar draws inspiration from the glamorous 1920s.

The grand salon features dazzling Murano glass chandeliers, a stunning marble bar, palm trees and coral-coloured walls, all adorned with bespoke illustrations. The atmosphere is quite relaxed, with comfy sofas and a cosy fireplace.

As for the cocktails, the menu during our last visit took us on 'The Great Irish Tour', with a man on a bicycle circling the Emerald Isle, following the poets and tasting cocktails created with flavours of fourteen countries along the way. So yes, the bartenders can definitely get quite creative with their drinks. A lovely venue to meet friends in for that post-work drink.

Coupette

THE BEST LITTLE COCKTAIL BAR IN EAST LONDON

⊖ Bethnal Green

Not in the fanciest of London's neighbourhoods, this little cocktail bar is for those in the know. Coupette is an unpretentious yet sophisticated bar in Bethnal Green that plays live music every evening. The space is intimate with low lighting, exposed brick walls and French touches here and there. It's the kind of place where it's the cocktails that do the talking rather than the fancy interiors.

Talking about cocktails, the menu often takes on different and interesting subjects. During our last visit, the menu was based on the world of street art, which, just like alcohol, was once prohibited. To put it together, Coupette collaborated with six local artists, with the job of creating murals that represented the cocktails (the kind of thing you only get in east London!).

Coupette is so popular that it also opened a second bar in Soho, Atelier Coupette, which is even smaller than this one and, like its sister bar, serves French-inspired cocktails and small dishes.

+ INSIDER TIP
〰〰〰〰〰〰

We definitely recommend trying the signature champagne Piña Colada: you won't have tasted anything like it yet!

Fitz's Bar

THE THEORY OF COLOUR

⊖ Russell Square

Located in the stylish Grade II-listed Kimpton Fitzroy, this Gatsby-ish hotel bar is the perfect place to escape the everyday. Just so you don't get confused, Fitz's Bar features two main areas: the Mural Room for walk-ins and perfect for an aperitif or glass of wine, and the glamorous Mirrorball Room, which is reservation only.

The Mirrorball Room is probably one of our favourite bars in London, thanks to its Jazz Age giant mirror ball, Art Deco-scalloped armchairs, ostrich feathers, magnificent eighteenth-century stained-glass window and impressive fireplace. Come 6 p.m., the lights go down and the jazz music goes up, and the only way to read the cocktail list is through a mini-UV flashlight. Talking about the cocktail list, it is no less impressive than the décor. On the Theory of Colour menu, each cocktail is based on fourteen altered versions of the 1660 artwork *Vase of Flowers* by Nicolaes van Verendael. The UV light we mentioned above helps you reveal hidden secrets on each page about what your choice of cocktail tells you about yourself as a person.

Fitz's Bar is definitely worth visiting if you love decadent interiors, interactive menus and an intimate setting.

One Hundred Shoreditch

A TASTE OF CALIFORNIA IN BUSY SHOREDITCH

Old Street/
Shoreditch High Street

The rooftop bar at One Hundred Shoreditch takes inspiration from Palm Springs, and it really is a little oasis in east London. Expect succulents and cacti, pink marble and – of course – panoramic views over the city. The cocktails and food menu are inspired by California, meaning you will find variations of Margaritas, coconut and pineapple spritzes and rosés, to be paired with dishes such as devilled eggs, guacamole, tacos, corn ribs and fried chicken.

The DJ plays Latin American music, making it a vibrant and fun summer hangout, especially for locals and hipsters (rather than the City's 9–5 crowd). It's a great spot for some spontaneous drinks on a sunny day, but if you do book, you will only be able to book a table inside – the terrace is walk-ins only.

Gordon's Wine Bar

LONDON'S OLDEST WINE BAR

Charing Cross/
Embankment

Established by Arthur Gordon in 1890, Gordon's, just minutes from the Embankment, is almost certainly London's oldest wine bar. It is a family affair, but the Gordon family who has been running the bar since 1975 is not related to Arthur. It's just a happy coincidence!

The iconic bar is minutes away from the Strand and Leicester Square, situated on Villiers Street between Charing Cross and Embankment stations. Yet, in all the hustle and bustle, it is somehow easy to miss if you don't know it's there. The inside of the bar is arguably the most romantic spot in London, absolutely perfect for a first date. Think old oak barrels filled with sherries and port, candlelit tables, newspaper clippings of historic events and old photographs. And, of course, all this while enjoying glasses of rare wines and cheeses.

The outdoor seating area on the other hand is always buzzing. Despite it being in a very touristy area, Gordon's is generally packed with Londoners gossiping away over Bordeaux and Barolo.

Sky Garden

LONDON'S HIGHEST PUBLIC GARDEN

Cannon Street

You haven't been to London if you haven't been to the Sky Garden. And that is how popular this rooftop is. Built on 20 Fenchurch Street (for many the Walkie-Talkie), in 2004, by world-renowned architect Rafael Viñoly, Sky Garden is London's highest public garden and has the almost unique feature of having a 360-degree view of the city. The Shard, St Paul's Cathedral, The London Eye, Canary Wharf – you see it all.

The space is very vibrant, with live bank and DJ nights adding to the atmosphere. As for the garden, the designers opted for a variety of drought-resistant plants from the Mediterranean and South Africa, so that they are always vibrantly green.

Entry is free, but you will probably need to book well in advance. Alternatively, you can book for one of the restaurants or bars. The Fenchurch Restaurant serves British fine dining food, while the Darwin Brasserie is more casual and has a lovely summer terrace during the warmer months. If not, you can just book a table for one of the great cocktails here with a view at the Sky Pod Bar.

Netil 360

HACKNEY'S SECRET GARDEN

⊖ London Fields

Set on top of Netil House, an old refurbished 1960s office block, Netil 360 is by many considered Hackney's secret garden. Popular with east Londoners, this unfussy rooftop bar has lovely panoramic views over London's skyline. So lovely that it has even been used for photoshoots by the likes of Dior and British Airways.

The interiors are very homely, the perfect spot to try their 48-hour fermented Neapolitan pizza, while the outside is vibrant and fun, with people mingling over spritzes, global wines and local craft beers from Five Points Brewery and spirits from the East London Liquor Company. And once the sun is down, the party really starts, especially on Fridays and Saturdays when there is a live DJ.

+ INSIDER TIP
〰〰〰〰〰〰

Want to know a little secret? Just next door are the Rooftop Saunas, private cabins with City views, where you can unwind after a long, stressful day. They feature cool-down spaces, showers and cold-water plunge barrels. We would definitely recommend!

Boundary

AN EAST LONDON LOCALS' FAVOURITE

Old Street

Boundary is set in a former Victorian warehouse, and is now a boutique hotel in one of London's most fashionable streets. It's one of those places that you either know is there or don't – making it a popular spot with locals.

This rooftop bar and restaurant features a large outdoor terrace and glass orangery that allows beautiful panoramic views over Shoreditch and a great place to watch a sunset, with one of the great cocktails like the Patron Silver-based Mexican or a glass of something delicious from the extensive wine and bubbly menu. The terrace gets a makeover in the cold months and becomes a beautiful winter terrace, with tastes from the Alpine regions, such as cheese fondue and melting raclette. While during summer, expect to see olive trees.

The outside lounge space is walk-ins only, so worth going early on warmer days.

E
V
E
N
I
N
G

Dukes Bar

SHAKEN NOT STIRRED – THE BEST MARTINI IN LONDON?

⊖ Green Park

Every true Londoner has been at least once to Dukes Bar to try Alessandro Palazzi's Vesper Martini. It's where we send our friends when they visit and ask us where they can drink the best Martini in London.

The Dukes Hotel is one of the most iconic hotels in London. It has seen many illustrious guests, from Oscar Wilde and Lord Byron to Frédéric Chopin and Edward Elgar. But perhaps the most famous guest to have stepped into this bar is Ian Fleming, known for his James Bond series of spy novels. It is said that after seeing its elegant, beautiful interior, he thought of it as the ideal place for Bond to enjoy a drink. There are different tales relating to Fleming at the Dukes Bar, most of them claiming that here is where he created the iconic Vesper Martini, which is what we order every time we go.

This drink is made of gin, one part vodka and half a measure of the French liqueur Lillet. It's very strong and normally you won't be served more than two, because otherwise the staff may have to carry you out!

+ INSIDER TIP
〜〜〜〜〜

Dukes Bar is open Monday to Saturday 3 p.m. to 11 p.m. You can book a table if you are a guest at the hotel but it's walk-in only for external guests, so better go early if you can.

The Little
Scarlet Door

THE PERMANENT HIDDEN
HOUSE PARTY

⊖ Leicester Square/
Tottenham Court Road

If you are walking along Greek Street in Soho, you may spot a huge red door. No indication of what may be inside, apart from a blue plaque dedicated to 'The Flatmates'. Bizarre, right?

What if we said that inside is a permanent hidden house party? The Little Scarlet Door is a bar that is meant to look like a New York loft apartment. As soon as you walk in, you will see sofas, houseplants, a Smeg fridge, a colander, a spice stack and anything else you would expect to see in someone's kitchen or living room. If you move downstairs, you will also find a washing machine, laundry detergent and a shower room filled with rubber ducks.

The cocktail menu reads as if you were scrolling through Netflix. You will see Kill Bill, Mad Men, Sex and the City or La-La Land. Some are served in a chilli tin, others served in a milk bottle. The Little Scarlet Door makes for a fun night out with friends, and it gets especially busy on Friday and Saturday nights when the house party goes into full swing, with DJs, long queues and interesting characters.

E
V
E
N
I
N
G

The American Bar at The Savoy

TIMELESS COCKTAILS IN AN ICONIC SPOT

⊖ Charing Cross

Ah, if those walls could speak! Nestled in what is one of our favourite hotels in London, the American Bar at the Savoy, opened in 1893, is the oldest standing American Bar in the world. Over the years, some illustrious guests have frequented the bar: think Marilyn Monroe, Frank Sinatra, Elizabeth II and Ernest Hemingway, just to mention a few. And, of course, Winston Churchill was a regular; so much so that he had his very own private whisky, which the bartender kept locked behind the bar for him.

In its long history, it has only had fourteen head bartenders, who have all left their mark in some way. The most famous was surely Harry Craddock, who left America during Prohibition and sailed to England with his family in 1920. After working for ten years at the American Bar, he put together the iconic the *Savoy Cocktail Book*, which is still sold today.

But enough about the history.

Today, stepping into the American Bar gives you that feeling of old world glamour, with a pianist playing Chopin, Debussy and Sinatra, while drinking timeless cocktails such as the White Lady, in the very bar where it was invented, in 1919.

As you can imagine, this bar is very popular, so we would definitely recommend booking in advance, maybe for after-theatre drinks or a romantic date.

The American Bar at the Stafford

ENJOY THE GLAMOUR
OF A BYGONE ERA

Green Park

Nestled in a quiet street in St James's and part of the Stafford hotel, the American Bar is one of the oldest and longest surviving American bars in London. During the 1930s, luxury hotels tried to appeal to high society with US-style cocktails and a relaxed but opulent ambience, and when you walk in here it really feels as if you have stepped into a bygone era.

The ceiling and the walls are filled with ties, model airplanes, signed photos of famous residents and lots of historical artefacts. The cocktails are St James's themed and served in showy glassware, while the ambiance is sophisticated and very old money. It's the perfect spot to impress someone visiting you in London, as it's so well hidden that only a true Londoner would know about it.

We adore the interiors, as you can tell, but there is also a beautiful terrace for those warm summer days.

E
V
E
N
I
N
G

The Red Room

THE SEXIEST BAR IN LONDON

⊖ Bond Street

Imagine walking through a hidden velvet curtain into a secret hideaway of an eclectic art collector's home. That is exactly the feeling you will get when entering the Red Room at the Connaught Hotel.

This rather unique bar is named after its collection of red artworks, all created by four female visionaries. The focal point of the room is the central marble fireplace, with *I Am Rouge* hanging above it, a striking work in watercolour, gouache and pencil by renowned artist Louise Bourgeois.

The Red Room is a luxury wine and art bar, with wines from the hotel's 30,000 bottle cellar, which includes obscure vintages and first growths brought in on a custom-made marble trolly. Even the cocktails have a touch of wine, all put together with seasonal ingredients at the stunning pink onyx bar by the creative bartenders.

The atmosphere is intimate, sexy and sophisticated, the perfect place to finish a date night.

K Bar

OLD MONEY VIBES IN KENSINGTON

⊖ South Kensington

Nestled within the Kensington Hotel in one of London's most charming 'hoods, K Bar is a sophisticated cocktail bar with an elegant old-money décor. We wouldn't be surprised if walking in you might think you were in an old-school private members' club. But no worries, here no one will ask you for your membership number in order to choose a drink!

If the warm oak panels, mirrored walls and glittering chandeliers aren't enough to convince you to pay a visit to K Bar, maybe the creative cocktails and savvy bartenders will do the trick. Its latest cocktail menu is presented in a reflective jewel box, where you can only read the menu from the reflection in the mirror. There is an extensive list of signature cocktails, but the bartenders are happy to put something together based on your tastes.

If you are not a cocktail person, don't worry, this also a great spot for a glass of red wine or champagne. With snacks like wild mushroom arancini and dressed Dorset crab brioche, from the Town House Kensington's restaurant kitchen, of course.

The Italians

The Italians is a cosy family-run wine bar located on a side street in Marylebone. The name itself suggests a great sense of community and, indeed, it's very popular with those people who live in this gorgeous part of town. The interiors help give that homely feeling, with lampshades that resemble Prosciutto, a bar handmade with Mount Etna lava stones, and around six thousand bottle corks hanging from the ceiling, with vintage Italian movie pictures hanging on the walls.

As for the wines, you will find varieties from all over Italy, with a dozen by the glass that change every few weeks, so that wine lovers can try different types. The team mentioned that they spent years visiting small producers around Italy to put together the list, in the process trying to create a big family, between them, the producers and the customers. How lovely!

The menu is quite simple and if you're not heading off for supper elsewhere, you can enjoy bruschetta, cheese and salami boards, grissini, focaccia, and mozzarella di bufala from Barlotti family in Campania.

The Artesian Bar

A FOUR-TIME
WINNER OF THE
WORLD'S BEST BAR

Oxford Circus

You open the cocktail menu and you see ingredients such as chicory, leek, kaffir leaves, insects and soil. Nope, you haven't walked into some sort of bougie farmers' market, you are actually at the world-famous Artesian Bar at the Langham hotel.

A four-time winner of the world's best bar, it is situated on the north end of Regent Street by John Nash's All Souls Church, and is known for getting really inventive with its cocktails. The Artesian Bar uses 'ingredients of the future', which are elements that are important for our planet, to put together the most creative and surprising drinks. We admit we were very sceptical about Insects, whose ingredients feature crickets and chicatanas, but we swear that after trying it we changed our minds.

Crickets aside, the Artesian Bar is worth visiting even only for its interiors, with the bar a nod to a Victorian cabinet of curiosities, the purple leather seating and the antique gold chandeliers on the ceilings.

This really is the perfect spot to unwind after a day out shopping on Oxford Street and Regent Street.

E
V
E
N
I
N
G

Wagtail

WATCH THE WORLD GO BY FROM A ROOFTOP BAR

⊖ Cannon Street

Sitting just north of the river near the Monument to the Great Fire of London, Wagtail is probably one of the most luxurious rooftop bars and restaurants in London. The space is split over two floors: the first the restaurant and the second the rooftop terrace bar. There is also a stunning private dining room called the Cupola, which comes with a bird's eye view of the river.

This rooftop is perfectly placed to be a great hangout for afterwork drinks, especially for City workers after a day of business meetings and closing deals. The heated outdoor terrace has a retractable roof, making it a joy to be on in all weathers, with views over Tower Bridge, St Paul's Cathedral, the Shard, the Gherkin and the Walkie-Talkie Building.

+ INSIDER TIP

Be sure to sit outside, facing London Bridge, and watch the world go by over a glass of wine or champagne, along with a few snacks from the bar menu.

The Painter's Room

ONE OF THE PRETTIEST BARS IN LONDON

⊖ Bond Street

When you walk into the Painter's Room at Claridge's hotel, you really feel as if you have just uncovered a secret location. We had been many times over the years to the dark and glamorous Fumoir and the iconic Claridge's Bar, but when we discovered this pastel pink bar, we instantly fell in love.

The Painter's Room is a small, intimate bar, the design influenced by 1930s photos from the hotel archives and a modern interpretation of the hotel's iconic Art Deco interiors. At the centre of the room is the stunning pink marble bar, surrounded by a mural of mischievous characters mingling by British artist Annie Morris, who also designed the stain-glass centrepiece of the room.

The cocktails are excellent and inspired by the artists, the flavours and shifting shades of southern Europe, but for us this is the perfect spot to sip a glass of champagne while listening to the live piano music.

International Hidden Gems

London's diverse foodie scene is something we're all familiar with now. There are all kinds of cuisines in this book, but here are some of our own personal international favourites, worthy of a mention.

ROTI KING

Malaysian street food star Roti King has become quite famous on the foodie scene, thanks its flaky and buttery roti canai, which, since its beginning in a not-so-pretty store in Euston, has been attracting daily long queues. And it's all about the food. After opening three (much prettier) branches in Battersea, Spitalfields and Waterloo, it has become wildly popular with city audiences. The idea: two pieces of roti come with a choice of 'kari': either fish, meat or dahl. You can also go for murtabak, roti stuffed with spinach and cheese, chicken or lamb. Wash it down with a hot (or cold) Teh Tarik, a traditional Malaysian pulled tea. In addition, Roti King serves a selection of rice and noodle dishes and desserts.

DELAMINA KITCHEN

With locations in Marylebone and Shoreditch, Delamina Kitchen showcases an eastern Mediterranean home-cooked-style of food with a strong Televivian flair, influenced by co-founder Lima's upbringing. Concentrating on the use of vegetables, grilling and roasting are the core methods of cooking. Trust us when we say everything is absolutely delicious, but don't miss out on the fluffy Sabich-style pita with double dips of smokey aubergine and tahini, and the house classic of crispy rosemary potatoes with garlic-infused yoghurt. On the dessert side, you must try the parfait of halva with roasted almonds and tahini drizzle and the kadayif nest of vanilla cheesecake cream with caramelised pecans. You won't be disappointed.

FATT PUNDIT

Originating from the Kolkata (Calcutta) in West Bengal, this particular cuisine originated when the Hakka people migrated from the Chinese province of Canton to India, creating an Indo-Chinese fusion food popular in the region. Named Fatt Pundit after the common Chinese surname and 'pundit' meaning scholar, the first branch in Soho has now translated to another branch in Covent Garden. Must-order dishes are the momo-steamed dumplings (with a veggie, fish or meat filling) which are at the start of every meal in Tangra. The crackling spinach with yogurt and pomegranate and the popcorn cauliflowers are also unmissable. For mains, order the monkfish curry with fresh coconut, and for dessert the sizzling brownie with ice cream is really what you should focus on. We do.

THE AFGHAN KITCHEN

Probably the best Afghan restaurant in London, this unpretentious but cute restaurant in Islington will give you a taster to a cuisine most of us have never tried before. At this bustling locale, seats are at a premium, so grab one when you can. What you're in for: one of the best cheap eats in London. Vegetables are the star of the show – with soft aubergine, thick moong dhal, tantalising slabs of pumpkin drizzled in yoghurt and warming stews boiling away temptingly in the kitchen. Our best tip: come as a group, so you can sample all the dishes on the menu – and, yes, you do have to share everything!

LUSIN

Head to this snazzy spot in Mayfair to try fine-dining Armenian food. Expect dishes like manti (steamed dumplings with meat, yoghurt and tomato sauce), kebabs and loads of pomegranate-infused dishes. To start, try Lusin's signature eggplant rolls with walnuts

and whipped cheese or the Luisin kibbeh with bulgur, meat and nuts. To finish, order the Luisin delicate rose-flavoured ice cream with cotton candy or the Armenian cheese maamoul with walnut ice cream. Perfect for a date night discovering each other and new flavours, too.

IKOYI

This sub-Saharan West African Michelin-starred restaurant in St James's will blow your mind. Ranked currently at no. 35 in the World's Best Restaurants, it has a kitchen based around its own specially sourced spices and British micro-seasonality. The menu has previously featured such wonders as jollof rice and crab custard, suya tamari pork with mustard greens and kumquat, and a flower sugar cake with batak berry and Garigette strawberry. While the décor of the restaurant is as pretty as the food, bear in mind this is not an easy one on your wallet. It's one for a special occasion, but, my, is it worth it.

JIKONI

This pastel-hued restaurant in Marylebone is inspired by immigrant cuisine and the shared flavours and cultural diversity of South Asia, the Middle East, East African and Britain. This mixed-heritage food results in a delicious home-cooked-style of food, inspired by recipes passed down through generations. The result, blended dishes featuring such lovelies as kale chaat, soy keema buns, okra fries and a pressed shoulder of Cornish lamb.

EVENING

DINNER

Akoko

MICHELIN-STARRED WEST
AFRICAN FOOD

 Goodge Street

When it comes to West African food in London, you really can't get better than Michelin-starred Akoko in Fitzrovia. Founder Aji Akokomi and executive chef Ayo Adeyemi bring together dishes mainly from Nigeria, Ghana and Senegal, drawing on exceptionally unique flavours and family recipes and turning them into fine dining. It's a real cultural and culinary voyage, and we can guarantee that you won't taste anything like this anywhere else in London!

We really loved the terracotta walls and African art throughout the restaurant, together with the live fire cooking and blend of seasonal British ingredients with exotic and possibly lesser known African spices. The restaurant serves a tasting menu only for both lunch and dinner, with a reduced option for lunch if you still want to try the experience but don't want the full menu. In terms of food, expect to see dishes like Gambian stew, plantain mossa, fish yassa and jollof rice.

We really loved the Akoko pairing, which combines ingredients, cocktails and wines from across Africa, rather than a classic wine pairing that you might expect to see in a Michelin-starred restaurant.

E
V
E
N
I
N
G

177

INO

CHARCOAL-COOKED GREEK FOOD IN CARNABY

⊖ Oxford Circus

INO is a Greek taverna-inspired restaurant on Newburgh Street, just off bustling Carnaby Street. The restaurant is influenced by the Greek culinary heritage of cooking over charcoal, meaning that all the dishes are grilled in the restaurant's open kitchen before being served. The interiors are unfussy and there is a long counter with red stools, which is the best spot in the house, where you can observe the chefs using hot charcoal to prepare most dishes, with occasional theatrical flashes of flame.

As for the food, the chefs only use a small number of ingredients that are all of the highest quality to cook their traditional dishes, all served to suit the modern aesthetic. The taramas, for instance, are shaped into pretty florets, topped with gelatinous orange garnish and cured cod's roe, and finished with an egg yolk to mix in. The traditional spanakopita pastry pie is layered like a mille-feuille, filled with spinach and barrel-aged feta from Athens, a cheese recipe almost one hundred years old and handmade from free-grazing sheep. The cheese is used in many INO dishes.

What is also barrel-aged are the cocktails, but you will probably want to focus more on the exceptional Greek wines, all available by the glass so that you can try more than one!

Finish the experience with the kaimaki ice cream made from sheep's milk, which is complemented by the taste of mastic from the island of Chios, which lends a subtle pine-like aroma and a hint of herbal sweetness to the ice cream. Delicious.

Bacchanalia

MAYFAIR OPULENCE AT ITS BEST

⊖ Hyde Park Corner/Marble Arch

Bacchanalia in Mayfair is like no other restaurant in London. Or in the world, really. Think two thousand-year-old Greek and Roman artworks, five enormous Damien Hirst sculptures – two unicorns, a winged lion, Medusa and Bacchus – flying above the tables, hand-painted ceiling murals and waiters greeting you dressed in togas. And all this put together at the modest cost of £75 million. There is no place like this: be certain about that.

With the above in mind, we really won't blame you if your jaw drops to the ground as soon as you walk into this opulent restaurant, which used to be a Porsche showroom. It's one of the few places you would forgive if the food and drinks weren't to the same standard as the interiors, as it's worth going just to be surrounded by so much decadence.

Fortunately, though, the food delivers. Surprisingly, the Greek–Italian inspired dishes are quite simple in contrast to the over the top décor. Expect to see tzatziki and baba ganoush with crudités, tuna tartare, beef carpaccio, Roman flatbreads, grilled octopus and abundant Greek-style salads to start, with truffle tagliatelle, salt-crust sea bass and wood-fire meats as mains, while to finish tiramisu, soft serve yogurt or half-baked chocolate cookies tempt.

One thing you shouldn't also miss are the opulent toilets. The men's are in inspired by Hades' underworld, where you are immersed in scenes of snakes and bulls, while the ladies are inspired by the Garden of Hesperides, with orchard greenery, flowers, nymphs and mosaics.

E
V
E
N
I
N
G

L'Oscar
Restaurant

PARISIAN
ELEGANCE
IN A FORMER
CHURCH

Holborn

Within L'Oscar in Holborn, a charming boutique hotel set in the former headquarters of the Baptist Church, lies L'Oscar Restaurant, which is styled to make you feel as if you are in a sophisticated and charming Parisian café.

Think of an illuminated onyx bar with ceilings lined with mirrors, gilded panels, stunning pieces of art and plush seating. The bar is so pretty that it would be ill-mannered not to start dinner with a cocktail or champagne served by the savvy bartenders, right? Moving on to the food, the menu is rather interesting. There is an eclectic mix of cuisines, from Mediterranean classics such as burrata, salad niçoise and truffle rigatoni, to Japanese delicacies like tuna tartare, crispy rice and salmon and a beautifully presented black cod. And we have to say, the Japanese crudos really steal the show.

To finish, the vanilla and hazelnut mille-feuille and dark chocolate and coffee namelaka are a must, paired with a glass of tokaji or saké.

The Clove Club

🚇 Old Street/Shoreditch High Street

If you have ever googled 'best restaurants in London', then it's likely that in the many lists present on the world wide web you will have often stumbled on The Clove Club. So what is so special about this restaurant so often featured in the World's 50 Best Restaurants? Many, many things.

Set behind the glossy blue door of Shoreditch's old town hall, two Michelin-starred The Clove Club has been a gamechanger ever since its opening back in 2013. Chef Isaac McHale's dishes are inspired by his many travels and have always used ingredients from the British Isles. This may be a common feature in London's foodie scene right now, but back when the restaurant opened it was an absolute novelty. And the precision with which these dishes are delivered is absolutely remarkable.

Each creation is treated like a piece of art, as you can tell by the presentation, taste and explanation by the knowledgeable servers. The ambience is laid-back, with a blue-tiled dining room and open kitchen that really make you feel at ease – just what you expect when dining out in east London.

The Clove Club only serves tasting menus, with a lighter version for lunch, and the menu changes constantly based on what is available on the market. The price is quite steep as you would expect from a two Michelin-starred restaurant. But boy is it worth it!

E
V
E
N
I
N
G

181

The Aubrey

⊖ Knightsbridge

The Aubrey is an izakaya-style restaurant nestled within the splendid Mandarin Oriental Hyde Park. Izakaya are usually informal bars that serve drinks and snacks in Japan, but as you would expect this is a five-star version of a late-night one.

You enter through Japanese cloth curtains into a wood-panelled bar, with the feeling that you have just uncovered a secret. In typical omakase-style there is no set menu, with cocktails moving with the seasons and being tailored to your taste. There is also a long list of aged and limited-edition sakés and Japanese whiskeys.

In the dining area, you will find velvet seating surrounded by over 250 pieces of Japanese art. Art is also referenced in the cocktail menu, with drinks themed around Art Nouveau artist Aubrey Beardsley, the inspiration for the restaurant name.

There is a long à la carte menu, but we tend to always go for the seasonal omakase menu, which includes some of Aubrey's best sellers, like the popcorn lobster, the wagyu dumplings, the miso black cod and – of course – the sushi platter, put together by the UK's only female sushi master Miho Sato. And that includes a yellowtail nigiri topped with ants (we all need our proteins, right?). There are DJs in the evening.

HUMO

FIRE DINING

 Oxford Circus

Michelin-starred HUMO is one of the most interesting restaurants in Mayfair, if not in London. Colombian-born executive chef Miller Prada uses neither gas nor electricity in his cuisine. Instead, his team cooks everything over a 4m (13ft) long wood-fired grill. And right in front of you. Humo means 'smoke' in Spanish, and each and every dish has a direct relationship with fire.

The design is dark and atmospheric, and the menu is divided into four categories: Ignite, Smoke, Flame and Embers, which represent the journey of fire. Chef Prada's Japanese influence is clearly visible, as most dishes are small and can be enjoyed with chopsticks. However, all the ingredients are rigorously sourced in the UK, and cooked and presented in the most precise way, taking into consideration ageing times, temperatures and the types of wood used.

We would recommend sitting at the counter to see all the process and passion that goes into the preparation of the dishes. Also, if you are looking for something even more special, book the chefs table, Abajo, where the chefs take the lead and give you the full HUMO experience.

Il Gattopardo

ALL STYLE AND SUBSTANCE

⊖ Green Park

Il Gattopardo – meaning 'the leopard' in Italian – is one of the most stylish Italian restaurants in town. The décor, the dishes, the drinks and the people.

Even though it's in one of the wealthiest neighbourhoods in London, there is hardly any pretentiousness about Il Gattopardo. The main room is full of mirrors, wood-panelled walls, old pictures and good vibes. You can even dine at the crudo bar for counter dining, or you can do just as we did and dine in the 'hidden' foliage-laden terrazza, with a retractable roof that opens during summer (the whole two weeks of it!).

Even though the interiors are very shiny, the cuisine is quite the opposite. The dishes are simple, mainly from the south of Italy, so no chicken alfredo parmigiana or cacio e pepe pizza (sorry, guys), but lots of spaghetti alle vongole, Genovese paccheri and traditionally made lasagna.

As per drinks, if you are a Negroni fan, as we are, then this is a dreamland for you. There are four different varieties, all made using a secret recipe.

Let's hope that this leopard doesn't change its spots anytime soon.

E
V
E
N
I
N
G

185

Jacuzzi

DECADENT
INTERIORS AND
PECORINO WHEELS

High Street
Kensington

Big Mamma group has taken London by storm in the past few years, with five fun, viby and incredibly decadent restaurants spread around London. Whether it's a Virgin Mary in the bathroom, extravagant – to say the least – cocktail glasses or see-through bathroom doors (but only from the inside, don't worry), they really have it all.

If we were forced to choose our favourite one though, it must be Jacuzzi in Kensington. The restaurant has three floors with décor influenced by the Renaissance and Venetian villas, full of Italian relics and Murano glass ornaments (and disco balls on the bathroom stairs, obviously). The food also doesn't disappoint, with the homemade focaccia, the pistachio burrata and the scenic spaghetti al tartufo served in a pecorino wheel a must. For dessert, we always order the choco jacquemousse, which is served directly from the tray.

Jacuzzi really makes for a fun night out with friends, especially at birthday parties where the 'Happy Birthday' celebrations from the staff can get – let's say – quite loud.

Baccalà

A TASTE OF THE ITALIAN SEA

⊖ London Bridge

We can say with confidence that Baccalà is the best Italian seafood restaurant in London, and we have tried quite a few. One of the most difficult things to find in this city is good seafood pasta dishes. Don't get us wrong, we have had some delicious lobster linguine, spaghetti con vongole and seafood paccheri, but they always seem to either be missing something or have ingredients that an Italian chef in Italy wouldn't consider.

Baccalà's dishes manage to make you feel almost as if you were on the Italian coast. Chef Moreno Polverini's attention to detail and quality ingredients are what make this cosy restaurant on Bermondsey Street so special. What we also love is that you will see familiar faces each time you visit, like sommelier and co-founder Fabio, who always helps us choose the best wines (the selection truly is stellar) and talks us through the wide selection of artisan extra virgin olive oils, which here are treated almost as preciously as wines.

Must-orders are the baccalà mantecato (whipped salt cod on polenta croutons), the la pentolaccia di chitarrine con sugo allo scoglio (chitarrine with seafood served in a copper pan) and the gnocchetti con vongole, friarelli e bottarga (gnocchi, clams, turnip tops and bottarga). The menu is more extensive in the evening, so we recommend going for a date night as the restaurant is cosy and intimate.

J Sheekey

THEATRELAND'S MOST LOVED
SEAFOOD RESTAURANT

⊖ Covent Garden

J Sheekey, in Covent Garden, is a restaurant filled with old-school glamour and timeless charm. It was opened in 1896, when local stallholder Josef Sheekey was given permission to serve fish and shellfish in St Martin's Court by Lord Salisbury on the condition that it would cater for the prime minister's post-theatre parties. Almost 130 years later, J Sheekey is still one of the most favoured restaurants in London's theatreland.

The interiors of this West End institution are very old-fashioned, with black and white pictures of famous actors on the walls and secluded tables. The staff wear white aprons and black waistcoats, which only adds to the charm of the place. The al fresco terrace is perfect for people-watching in the summer, where you will see a long line of people queuing for a show just around the corner.

As for the seafood, it's of the highest quality. The oysters, scallops and shellfish platters are as fresh as they come, while the fish pie holds a legendary status among diners. And if you have a sweet tooth, the baked pear tatin with vanilla ice cream is to die for, but these dishes do change with the seasons, so you may not find it on the menu all year round.

The River Café

THE ITALIAN
RESTAURANT
THAT MADE
PEASANT FOOD
FASHIONABLE

Hammersmith

Hammersmith's River Café opened in 1987 as a Tuscan-inspired restaurant. Soon after, founders Ruth Rogers and Rose Gray started to travel and discover more about Italy and slowly introduced more regional cuisine to the menu. At the time, most Italian restaurants in London would only serve heavy (and not very good) pizza and pasta dishes, so this was seen as a novelty, which has in the years gained them the reputation as one of the best and most celebrated Italian restaurants in London, training an eclectic and impressive range of chefs, with Jamie Oliver, Theo Randall and April Bloomfield among them.

River Café continues to show Londoners and foodies alike how varied and tasty Italian cuisine can be, and as a result it has held a Michelin star since 1998. The menu showcases dishes from different regions of Italy and the wine list has wine from every single region of Italy, many from small producers. The dishes change regularly, but what hasn't changed is the café's infamous chocolate nemesis cake, with the gelato also an absolute must-try.

The crowd may seem very relaxed, as is the vibe of the restaurant, but be sure to keep your eyes peeled, as you will quite often spot movie stars, artists and other celebrities.

If you decide to make your way to River Café, be sure to go on a sunny day and sit on the terrace overlooking the Thames.

EVENING

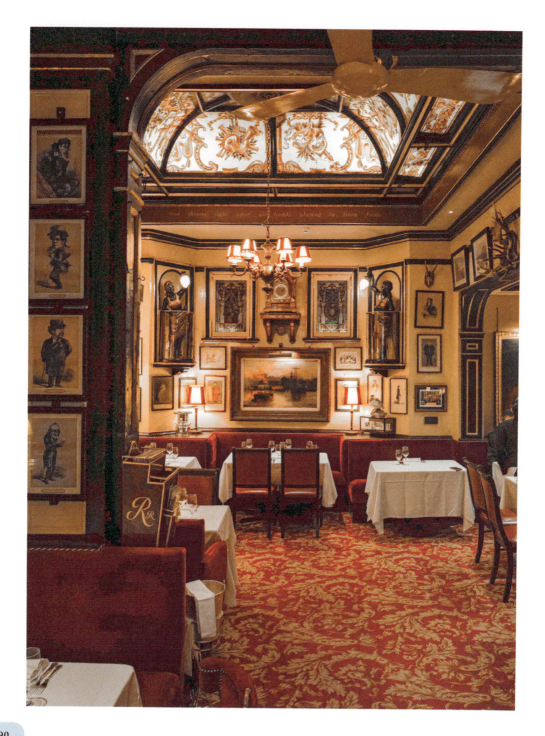

Rules

LONDON'S OLDEST-RUNNING
RESTAURANT

⊖ Covent Garden

In 1798, Napoleon commenced his campaign in Egypt, France began its two-year siege of Malta, the Society of United Irishmen instigated a major uprising against British rule in Ireland and the Europeans first discovered a very bizarre animal called the platypus. In addition to that, Thomas Rule decided to please his family and settle down after a life of excesses and open an oyster bar in Covent Garden called after himself, Rules.

Fast forward approximately two and quarter centuries and today Rules is London's oldest-running restaurant and one of the most celebrated in the world. This restaurant has survived nine monarchs, and has been crowded with artists, writers, actors and prime ministers, as well as featuring in many novels and films. It has only been run by three families, with Charles Rule, a descendent of the founder, Tom Bell, a Briton who owned a restaurant in Paris, during the First World War. Bell's daughter then sold the restaurant to John Mayhew, who owns it today.

Walking in almost feels like entering a museum, as you're surrounded by the black and white pictures, caricatures, antlers and paintings that adorn the walls. It has old-school charm. Rules serves British traditional food at its best, and it specialises in classic game cookery (the menu even states 'game birds may contain shot'), oysters, pies, roasts and puddings. The dessert options are also impressive, including golden syrup steamed sponge with custard, sticky toffee pudding and vanilla cheesecake with redcurrant compote on the menu. The only caveat is that there was not one vegetarian dish on the menu when we visited, so if you are vegetarian or vegan, this may not be the best place for you.

Rules is a special place that every Londoner should have on their bucket list, whether it's a special occasion, a casual business meeting or just to try out the oldest restaurant in London.

Le Cordon Bleu

THE WORLD'S BEST COOKING SCHOOL

Holborn

Founded in Paris in 1895, Le Cordon Bleu is considered to be one of the most prestigious networks of culinary and hospitality schools in the world, and of course there is also one in London, precisely in Bloomsbury.

In addition to training professional chefs, Le Cordon Bleu offers a number of short one-day classes or evening cookery courses that are both fun and educational. Whether you want to brush up your baking skills, learn to cook a dish you just tried in an exotic restaurant or learn how to perfectly pair your wines, there is definitely something for you.

The Culinary Voyage classes are superb, where chefs focus on a certain country to teach you some of its most iconic dishes. You are virtually transported away from rainy London for a few hours into a location of your choice. Think delicious Spanish, Brazilian, Lebanese and Mexican food. You will definitely impress your friends when you host next dinner.

This is the perfect gift for a foodie friend, or even to yourself. Why not?!

Manicomio

YOU MUST BE MAD
NOT TO GO HERE

Sloane Square

Manicomio, in Chelsea, is set in what was formerly the Duke of York Military Asylum, hence the name Manicomio, which is Italian for 'madhouse'. Today, it's one of the best spots to dine in the area, after a visit to the nearby Saatchi Gallery, some shopping on the King's Road or a walk through Chelsea's charming streets.

While the interiors are nice and cosy for wintertime, our favourite feature of Manicomio is the outdoor seated terrace, which is one of the best al fresco spots in southwest London, perfect for watching well-dressed locals walking by with their dogs while sipping a spritz and sharing some stuzzichini (small Italian plates).

The menu is very seasonal, meaning we have tried different dishes every time we've visited, but the main attraction has to be the carbonara, one of the best we have tried in London – no pre-made sauce used here!

E
V
E
N
I
N
G

Noci

Noci is our local neighbourhood go-to place in Islington. Whenever someone is visiting London and we want to impress them, or if a friend is visiting our 'hood, Noci is the place we retreat to. We're not too sure what it is about this restaurant that always makes us come back – maybe it's the affordable pasta dishes, the homely feel or the silk handkerchief pasta. It must be the latter.

Noci serves Italian dishes with a twist. It likes to play around with the ingredients. Consequently, the menu changes quite often. We have had at least five different twists on the handkerchief pasta, the only consistent part being the egg yolk in the middle. They tasted delicious every time. The only dishes that are always on the menu are the legendary Genovese ragu, with a scenic tableside serving of Tête de Moine cheese, and the brown butter cacio e pepe ziti.

Noci has been so popular in Angel that there are now sister restaurants in Shoreditch, Richmond and Battersea, but for us the original restaurant remains the most special.

Osteria Romana

A SLICE OF ROME IN LONDON

⊖ Knightsbridge

Osteria Romana is a little slice of Rome, situated in a narrow alleyway in wealthy Knightsbridge. You will probably have stumbled upon it while walking from Hyde Park to Harrods and thought that it looked really pretty, and if you have been to Rome, you probably said out loud: 'Oh this reminds me so much of Trastevere.'

This Italian restaurant serves typically Roman food. You kick off your dinner with the waiter cutting off a few leaves of basil from the fresh pot on your table and pouring olive oil on top, for you to dip your fresh focaccia in. Then you move on to ordering one of the very rich tasting dishes: cacio e pepe, Italian chicory, Roman-style gnocchi with truffle, spaghetti carbonara. Anything that tickles your fancy, really!

We always like to dine on the terrace when we can, but the interiors are equally beautiful, with terracotta walls, low lighting, vintage pictures on the wall and Italian music that gives you a little taste of La Dolce Vita.

Riviera

A TASTE OF THE SOUTH OF FRANCE SUNNY ST JAMES'S

⊖ Green Park

It's happened to all of us during those windy and drizzly London days (you know the ones!), where not even an umbrella and a raincoat help prevent you from getting soaked, and you dream about being on the golden beaches of sunny Provence. Riviera, in St James's, is as about as close as you can get to that in the capital.

Set in a Modernist building that used to house the *Economist*, Riviera virtually transports you to the South of France, with its rich Mediterranean flavoured cuisine, served in a relaxed yet luxurious ambiance. The interiors are just stunning. You arrive at the main dining area via the original escalator of the building, dating back to the 1960s. It's slow, but it gives you the time to admire the artwork that lines the walls, which is all from the personal collection of the owners, the Zandi brothers.

The main dining room is very bright and airy thanks to the floor-to-ceiling windows, and the first thing you notice is the stunning bar, with bartenders mixing drinks using the bottles that adorn it. The colours are an ode to the sandy beaches and azure water of the glamorous French Coast, and the menu features dishes such as the signature Riviera sandwich with smoked salmon, cream cheese and caviar, the ratatouille and feta cheese brioche, the turbot à la meunière, grilled lamb cutlets with puy lentils and the best-presented mash potatoes we have seen in London

Special mention has to go to the lavender crème brûlée and the apple tarte tatin, both must-orders and, as we know, absolutely to die for.

Scott's Richmond

PREMIUM SEAFOOD AND
ROMANTIC RIVER VIEWS

 Richmond

Sister of the iconic Scott's of Mayfair, this riverside restaurant, in charming Richmond, is just what was missing from London's foodie scene. After being greeted by a smart looking doorman, walking in feels as if you have just landed in *Great Gatsby* movie. Think Venetian crystal chandeliers, tall ceilings, colourful watercolour paintings, silver columns and, at the centre of the room, a gold island and raw bar for guests to enjoy seafood counter-style. All this with pretty pink stools.

The food is pretty similar to its Mayfair counterpart. Premium fresh seafood, oysters, lobster, crab served in its shell, monkfish tail, you name it. All sustainably sourced and from the British Isles, where possible. The desserts also certainly don't disappoint, with our go-to being the incredible Paris-Brest, filled with pistachio ice cream and finished with gold leaf. We watched, captivated, as our smartly dressed waiter poured hot chocolate sauce on top.

The interiors may be impressive, but what we absolutely love about Scott's Richmond, especially during summer, is the outdoor terrace on the first floor, with striking views over the River Thames, making for one of the most romantic spots in London.

Sucre

ARGENTINIAN
FIRE DINING

Oxford Street

Set in the iconic three-centuries-old building which was once the London College of Music, Sucre is the product of the collaboration between iconic Argentinian bartender Tato Giovannoni and chef Fernando Trocca, the former executive chef of the original award-winning Sucre in Buenos Aires.

The restaurant's interiors are breathtaking. The building's industrial features have been kept and the high ceilings are adorned with dramatic chandeliers made from over a thousand cut-glass decanters. There's also an open kitchen.

The menu is inspired by chef Trocca's immigrant background, featuring the rich flavours of Argentinian, Spanish and Italian cuisines. The fire dining includes dishes such as padron peppers with mojo rojo, wood-fire aged Cheddar and onion empanada, sweet corn ribs with lime, tajine and guajillo salt, and of course, fire-grilled fish and meat. Finish with the remarkable dulce de leche fondant, one of the best desserts we have had in London.

After (or before) dinner you should also definitely head to their speakeasy-style Alma Bar, for creative cocktails and good vibes.

Galvin
La Chapelle

AN EAST LONDON
DESTINATION
RESTAURANT

Liverpool Street

This Michelin-starred restaurant in Spitalfields by the iconic Galvin brothers is truly special. It's set with a Victorian Grade-II listed building, St Botolph's Hall, formerly a school chapel, and serves incredible modern French-inspired food, using bold flavours and fresh British ingredients, typical of the chefs' cuisine. Galvin La Chapelle also has the world's largest collection of Hermitage La Chapelle wines in the world. What more can you want, right?

The large arched windows, high stone ceilings and elegant interiors provide the perfect backdrop for a romantic date. The menu features dishes such as the Dorset crab raviolo, Landes white asparagus, Hereford beef Châteaubriand, Orkney scallops and Cornish cod.

As for dessert, a must is definitely the rum baba with golden raisin compôte and crème Fontainebleau, with the baba sliced at the table, soaked in rum, right in front of your eyes. The cheese trolley is also impressive, which again is expertly explained and served at your table.

EVENING

The Libertine

DINING IN
VAULTED
HISTORY

Liverpool Street/
Monument

If you have walked past the Royal Exchange many times and not once noticed the Libertine, well we really can't blame you, as we have done exactly the same thing. Once London's first purpose-built centre for trading stocks, the City of London's Grade-I listed building now hosts many eateries and shops, including the likes of Fortnum & Mason, Ladurée, Grind and Buns from Home, to mention a few. But this one here is something pretty special. The Libertine is – in fact – set in the vaults of the Royal Exchange, which once stored goods such as the spices and silks sold above. In 1571, Elizabeth I granted it royal status and a licence to serve alcohol, the first venue in Britain to be granted that.

As soon as you walk through the entrance you feel as if you have been transported to a different era. There's a vintage shop filled with equine-themed artefacts, an homage to Elizabeth I's love of horses.

Down the steps you walk into the main vault, which features a long bar full of City workers enjoying drinks. Next door is the restaurant which serves a brasserie-style menu. You will find seafood, steaks, lobster rolls, fish of the day and seasonal starters.

On Sundays, a traditional English roast is served, which we have heard is one of the best in London.

The Orrery

THE BEST CHEESE TROLLEY IN LONDON

⊖ Regent's Park

The Orrery is set in a beautiful converted nineteenth-century stables in charming Marylebone. The large arched windows with views over Marylebone Church Gardens, the secret rooftop terrace and the elegant interiors make this restaurant one of the best places to escape London's fast-paced life.

The menu is French, the food elevated but not pretentious; it has a 22-page wine list, many by the glass. You will find dishes such as asparagus with truffle dressing, egg yolk and Parmesan, and lobster ravioli with bisque and pea risotto, artichoke crisp and Parmesan on the menu. The desserts are seasonal, but the real showstopper is the farmhouse cheese from trolley.

The very savvy and rather eccentric cheese expert talks you through the different types of British, French and Italian cheeses, each one with an interesting and fun story. He even let us cut our own slices of Fontina, goat's cheese, Manchego and Stilton, while talking about how he grew up in French Caledonia. Once our plates were ready, the manager poured a glass of port from a giant bottle to complete the experience.

Clos Maggiore

A DREAMY SOUTHERN EUROPEAN-INSPIRED CULINARY LANDSCAPE

⊖ Covent Garden

Southern European-inspired Clos Maggiore in Covent Garden is, we think, one of London's most romantic restaurants. Walk inside this dreamy restaurant and it will seem to have been tailor-made for a date or a wedding proposal. It's an oasis of calm in a rather chaotic area of London, where couples can get cosy surrounded by the Provençal and Tuscan countryside-inspired interiors.

The cherry-blossomed-adorned conservatory is one of the best dining rooms in London (be sure to request a table there), with a retractable roof creating a bright and airy space in the summer, and candles and a crackling fire to make this one of the most intimate spots in winter. If that is not enough, during the festive season Clos is transformed into a beautiful winter wonderland.

As for the menu, it features French classics, champagne and an extensive wine list, with all dishes explained by the savvy French staff. Despite the southern European influence, the restaurant prides itself of using UK suppliers and seasonal locally grown products.

+ INSIDER TIP

The pricing is on the high side, but allow us to let you in on a little secret: Clos Maggiore offers very convenient lunchtime and pre-/post-theatre menus, so you can go for the vibe without breaking the bank.

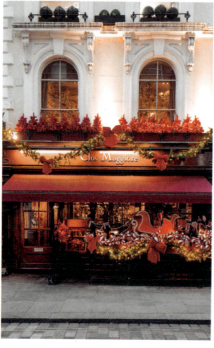

Little Italy Clerkenwell

Ⓔ Farringdon

As with Chinatown, every major city around the world has an Italian enclave, known as 'Little Italy'. Although a lot of people probably don't know it, the one in London used to be around Clerkenwell. While the area, as such, no longer exists, some interesting features and nods to Italian culture still remain including, of course, food.

Located between Rosebery Avenue, Clerkenwell Road and Farringdon Road, the neighbourhood was established when a new wave of skilled immigrants came over from northern Italy in the nineteenth century. The lack of jobs back home pushed them to seek better opportunities in London and this area, close enough to the City and the West End, became an area for craftmen and the perfect place for them to use their skills. By 1861, there were over 700 Italians living in the cramped streets of Clerkenwell.

The overcrowding occured when a second wave of immigrants, predominantly poor and desperate people from the south of Italy, arrived in the area. The two groups had little to do with each other, and while loud and sometimes rough, the second group also brought its food traditions with them. Luckily for us, they were largely responsible for introducing ice cream to the UK, filling Clerkenwell with ice cream stalls. At one point, half of the population of Little Italy were ice cream vendors, Ωsw2 and entrepreneur Carlo Gatti opened the first shop to sell ice cream to the public, making gelato and chocolate available to the average customer.

While criminality was common in the area, with Godfather figures such as the the fearsome Charles 'Darby' Sabini, Little Italy also attracted Giuseppe Mazzini, the famous political exile advocating for Italian unification. While living in the area he founded a social club, a free school for underprivileged Italian children and facilitated the building of the now Grade II-listed St Peter's Italian Church in Clerkenwell Road, giving Italians a place to worship. Modelled in a Basilica-style, this stunning church remains in use for Italian gatherings, and masses in their native language, especially at Christmas and Easter. Visit on the third Sunday of July to experience the procession in Honour of Our Lady of Mount Carmel that has taken place in the streets of Clerkenwell since 1896 and enjoy Italian delicacies from the stalls and vendors. Speaking of which, right next to St Peter's Church is Terroni, London's oldest Italian delicatessen, which opened in 1878. Today this is the place to go for ice creams and other Italian goodies not easily found in London. We love going for breakfast and watching all the 'nonnas' getting an early start on their groceries, buying the meats and cheeses for lunch, or popping by for a quick pasta lunch break in between work.

And while the Italian community developed and moved out of the area into what were more prosperous and diverse areas of London, you can still experience through its food and culture in what was once an important Italian area. For some of the most traditional Italian food you'll experience, head to the nearby Brutto, an acclaimed Florence-style trattoria with a Michelin Bib Gourmand. With white and red tablecloths, candlelit tables and incredible food, this is the perfect place to go with your amore.

+ INSIDER TIP
〰〰〰〰

If you're exploring the area, some of our other picks, including Exmouth Market and Luca (see page 70) are close by, and worth visiting.

1 EXMOUTH MARKET

2 BRUTTO

TERRONI & SONS

3

4 ST. PETER'S ITALIAN CATHOLIC CHURCH

5 LUCA

Farringdon

Barbican

Chancery Lane

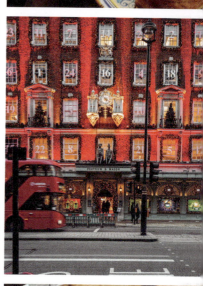

Quarto

First published in 2025 by Frances Lincoln
an imprint of The Quarto Group.
One Triptych Place, London, SE1 9SH
United Kingdom
T (0)20 7700 9000
www.Quarto.com

EEA Representation, WTS Tax d.o.o.,
Žanova ulica 3, 4000 Kranj, Slovenia

A catalogue record for this book is available
from the British Library.

ISBN 978-0-7112-9374-8
EBOOK ISBN 978-0-7112-9375-5
10 9 8 7 6 5 4 3 2 1

Book Designer: Nikki Ellis
Editorial Director: Jenny Barr
Publisher: Philip Cooper
Senior Commissioning Editor: John Parton
Senior Designer: Isabel Eeles
Senior Editor: Charlotte Frost
Senior Production Controller: Rohana Yusof

Printed in China

Acknowledgements

Who would have thought we would be here,
writing and publishing our third book when we
started our little Instagram page ten years ago.
Eating and drinking our way around London
has been a hard job but somebody had to do it!
A special thank you to:

Friends and family: Thank you so much for
continuous support though this journey, we
always strive to make you proud.

Our puppy Piccolo: Thank you for all the
cuddles when we were knees deep into
writing this book.

Our followers: Thank you to our beautiful
Instagram community for following us along,
without you we would not be where we are
now. Thank you to everyone that supported
us by buying our books thought the years, we
hope they still inspire you.

London's restaurants and bars: Thank you
for your enthusiasm in being part of this and
being so helpful and accommodating. You are
London's backbone and what makes this book
so special! A huge thank you to all the PR and
social media teams behind the venues for all
your help in organising our visits, we hope
you'll love the final result.

Publishing Team: Thank you so much to our
wonderful editors Charlotte and John and
all the team at Quarto for making this book
possible and for all your valuable insights.

Finally, thank you to everyone who purchased
and read this book – we hope we made you
hungry to discover London more!